EARTH TO SPIRIT

EARTH TO SPIRIT

In Search of Natural Architecture

DAVID PEARSON

Gaia Books Limited

A GAIA ORIGINAL

This book was written, illustrated and
photographed* by David Pearson

EDITORIAL	Michele Staple
DESIGN	Bridget Morley
DIRECTION	Joss Pearson
	Patrick Nugent

(* *All photographs by David Pearson except
those credited on page 159*)

This is a Registered Trade Mark of Gaia Books Limited

First published in the United Kingdom in 1994 by
Gaia Books, 66 Charlotte Street, London W1P 1LR

Printed and bound by Mandarin Offset, Hong Kong

A catalogue record for this book is available
from the British Library.

ISBN 1 85675 046 9

10 9 8 7 6 5 4 3 2

To Joss, for sharing the journey

Contents

The photographs on the preceding pages show:
AIR AND WATER: *rain-water mirror, Seoul, South Korea (P.2).*
EARTH AND FIRE: *"Horno" oven, Taos Pueblo, New Mexico (P.5).*
METAL AND WOOD: *antique door and knocker, Bologna, Italy (FACING PAGE).*
The photograph overleaf shows:
SENSE OF PLACE: *Theodoti, Ios, Greece.*

FOREWORD

Dwellings and buildings are meant to be lived in, to be enjoyed, to provide enchantment and psychic wellness for their users. This sounds so obvious as to be banal. Yet mainstream architecture seems propelled by greed (square-foot cost), personal ego (the charlatan's strut and self-indulgent posturings), and ideas awkwardly adapted from literary criticism, such as post-modern, deconstructivist, retro-nostalgic, neo-classic, and post-structuralist.

New approaches to making shelters and buildings are long overdue. Such directions appear out of real needs and social shifts, not from self-serving "statements" or "gestures" by celebrity-architects.

David Pearson has identified the development of such a new and emerging direction, one that is of enormous importance. He was among the earliest people in this country to recognize the profound role that buildings can serve in providing health as well as psychic and spiritual calm to those who live, work, or worship in them. His insights were described succinctly and well illustrated in his earlier book, *The Natural House Book*, which holistically viewed how to make homes benign again. He has now recognized more clearly the crucial need for ecologic and environmental sustainability, and that such green architecture must be nourished by an overarching spiritual commitment.

Harmony and balance, the archetypal sense of vernacular form, the relation of house to landscape through geomancy (*feng shui*) and context, *Baubiologie*, and the organic forms of Frank Lloyd Wright, all are examined and enriched by colour photographs that add to both the magic and visual beauty of the book. The humble villages of Hassan Fathy, the cultural diversity of dwellings and their functional and ritual usage, and the Rudolf-Steiner-inspired structures of a new hands-on generation of designer-builders are enriched by Pearson seeing them as a web of interconnected entities that explore the spiritual nature of space, time, and becoming.

David Pearson's writings are richly illustrated and develop the theme of green and gentle architecture through his vision of buildings fit for Gaia, a Yin and Yang of the spirit and the land. The book reveals the many decentralized efforts going on all over the world to return to ways of making homes that are meaningful, but draws up an exciting agenda for how we must think about architecture from here on.

My Navajo friends say "Live in balance and walk in beauty." A good summation of the spirit of this volume.

VICTOR PAPANEK
Author of *Design for the Real World*

December 1993

PREFACE

This book is the record of a personal odyssey – my search for architecture that is in harmony with nature. An odyssey that began with *The Natural House Book*, in which I explored three profound themes of natural architecture: ecology, health, and spiritual awareness. Since publication, *The Natural House Book* has evoked an enormous and enthusiastic response. It seemed to strike a deep and immediate chord with many people and to express for them a new vision – one for which they felt both sympathy and understanding, and that was practical enough for them to bring into their own lives and homes.

This response led me to found, with others, the Ecological Design Association – an ongoing network of architects and designers (SEE P.148) – and also to join with architects from many countries in forming Gaia International (ALSO P.148). At the same time, I was invited to visit and lecture in many parts of the world where exciting new things were happening. I began to travel and correspond widely to find (and photograph) more initiatives, large and small, which share this vision and to meet or contact the people who are pioneering them. They range from solar panels on cave houses, to whole permaculture communities, and large offices and banks. Many are produced on very tight budgets with self-build volunteers, while projects in developing countries are aimed at helping low-income and homeless people.

Some of the projects are very strong on ecology, some radical in health terms, some powerful spiritually. Very rarely do projects successfully combine and balance two or even all three elements. When they do, one can see a glimmer of a future that is coming! The enthusiasm and commitment of their creators, however, are impressive. For many, the experiences have changed their lives and have empowered them to go still further.

In this book, I invite you to share this odyssey and sample the excitement and hope of the new architecture. We start by going back to the spiritual roots found in *Ancestral Archetypes*. We go on to explore the rejuvenating quality of today's *Healing Architecture*, and the art of living and building with ecological awareness in *Harmony with the Land*. We experience some of the lessons of traditional building in *Vernacular Wisdom*, and move on to developing countries to witness their striving for *Cultural Identity*. Our journey ends with new beginnings by meeting some of today's pioneers involved in *Living the Dream*.

Enjoy the journey and make your link with earth to spirit.

INTRODUCTION

Over the last decade there has been an exciting change of direction in architecture, pioneered by a new generation of natural architects from many countries. All share a reawakening of consciousness for designing, building, and living that puts us back in touch with the earth and ourselves. This consciousness is as old as building itself, reaching back through ethnic traditions across the world. Our ancestors were more sensitive to their environment. They developed a particular sense of place and time, and knew the vital importance of honouring the primeval forces. Everywhere, indigenous building strove to express a harmony between people, land, and cosmos – to make forms that linked earth to spirit.

Our human world view is entering a period of massive change. There is a return to an understanding and respect for our links with the earth, the materials and artefacts we use. No longer is it acceptable to inhabit buildings (and cities) that make little or no reference to environmental issues or are patently bad for our health and wellbeing, let alone our spirit. Places like this – built out of the exploitation of the world's scarce resources, and/or polluting air, water, and land with their toxic wastes – are tantamount to a *rape* of the environment. Moreover, they are an assault on ourselves and our sensibilities.

But we do not have to spend our lives in such "post-rape environments" and bequeath them to our children. In many countries around the world a new architecture is emerging. An architecture that is synchronized with the natural forces around it and blends with the local ecosystem. An architecture that supports life and health and brings regeneration to body and soul. An architecture that puts us in touch again with the primeval forces of life – sun, wind, earth, and water – and celebrates the cycle of the seasons. An architecture that is respectful of nature, caring for health, and nurturing to the spirit – as architect Malcolm Wells has called it: *a gentle architecture*.

The new architecture has its roots deep in vernacular tradition, which is rich in messages that are becoming more and more relevant to our time – messages that help us to remember a humility and a belonging to the earth. And its scope is broad. Examples range worldwide, from healthy homes in Germany, built on *Baubiologie* principles, to exciting eco-cycle houses of the Gaia Group, Norway; from the new-ground-breaking projects of Bill McDonough and Paul Bierman-Lytle in North America, to the healing environments of Californian architect Carol Venolia. It spans the anthroposophic designs by followers of Rudolf Steiner's philosophy, including the *organic* architecture of Dutch architect Ton Alberts and the *Ökohaus* office in Frankfurt by Joachim Eble. It is also inspired by the stunning designs of world-famous Hungarian architect Imre Makovecz, and by the architects of the vernacular in developing countries, such as the late Hassan Fathy in Egypt and Charles Correa in India.

These are some of the pioneers who are forging the new agenda for an architecture fit for a civilized world to enter the 21st century.

The New York headquarters of the Environmental Defense
Fund was conceived by architect Bill McDonough as a
miniature university in a Greek city. At the centre, the
"Agora" encourages serendipitous encounters. In the
glossy black granite floor floats a bright globe – a constant
reminder of earth consciousness (SEE ALSO P.23).

The dome – a classic archetype. Springing skyward and defying earthly gravity, the dome symbolizes the heavens and cosmos above. It transports us from earth to heaven; from earth to spirit.

The same desire for uplifting release inspires the magnificent modern timber dome interior from the meeting hall of the Lutheran church, Siófok, Hungary, by world-renowned architect Imre Makovecz (RIGHT).

The simple, yet perfect Byzantine dome of brick and tile mosaic (ABOVE) crowns the small church at the 11th-century monastery of Hosias Loukas, not far from Delphi, Greece.

OVERLEAF: Sacred buildings provide a home for spiritual powers and ceremonial practices. Angels soar above the altar of Makovecz's Roman Catholic church at Paks, Hungary (LEFT), reaching toward the light.

Through ritual dances and dream songs, the native American roundhouse (OVERLEAF, RIGHT) offered participants a vehicle to communicate with their spirit world.

"There above, there above,
At the mystical earthlodge of the south.
Spirits are wafted along the roof and fall.
There above, there above."

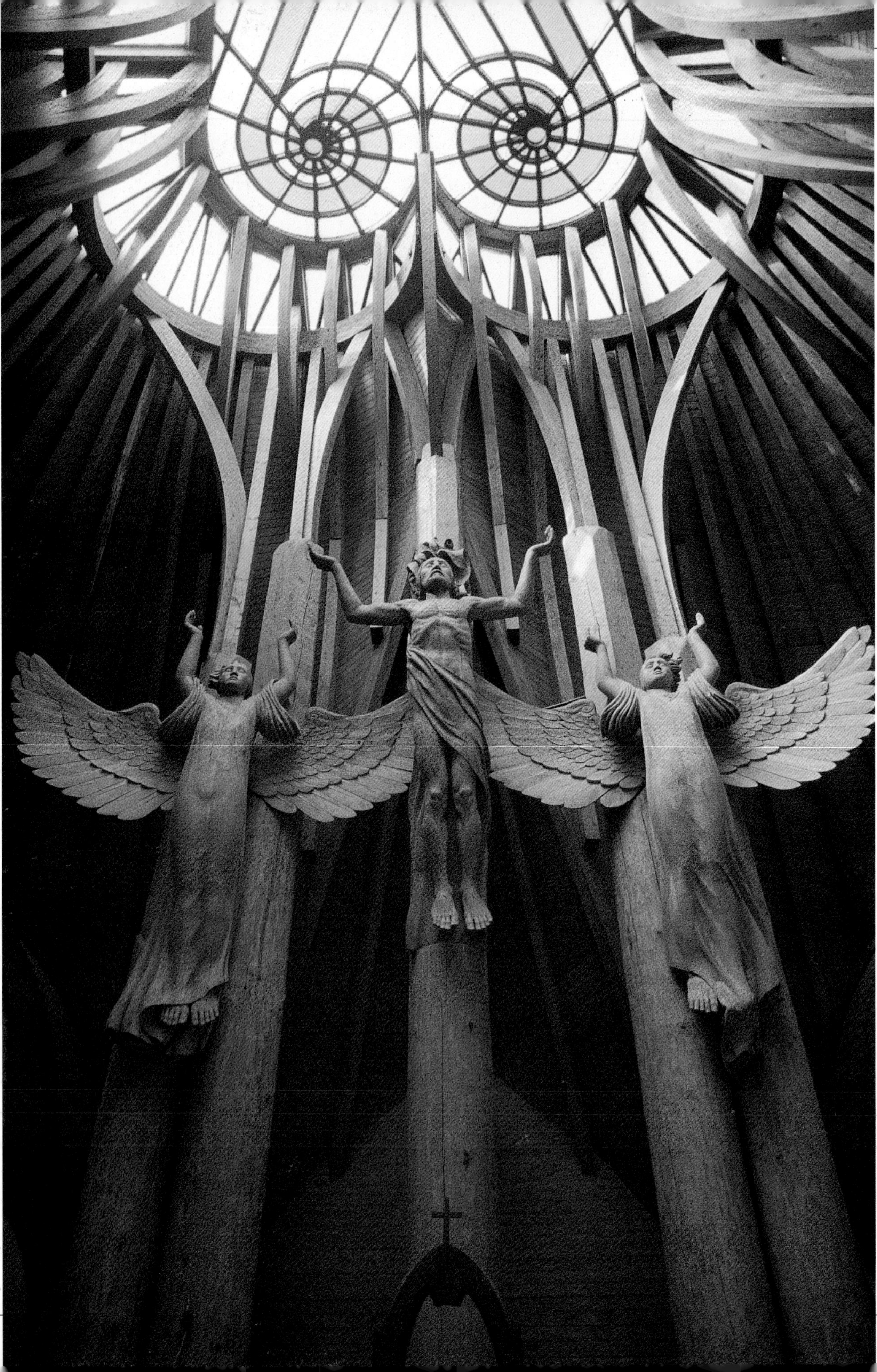

The perfect expression of the courtyard.

Cool and peaceful in Mykonos town, Greece.

LEFT: *Steiner kindergarten at Nant-y-Cwm, Dyfed, Wales by Christopher Day. According to Day: "Non-rectangular spaces are more life enhancing both inside and outside. But they are much harder to work with as enclosures of place – harder but possible. The issue is not between rectangles and non-rectangles: why do something differently from the normal unless there is good reason? The issue is between living and lifeless forms and spaces, life-renewing and life-sapping environments."*

ABOVE: *What could have been just another ordinary straight fence and rectangular gate has become a flowing, harmonious, and life-enhancing design around architect Jonathan Yardley's home at Ganges, British Columbia, Canada. Note how saplings cut from the site have been integrated into the gate design and holes cut in the fence allow branches to continue to grow through!*

ABOVE: *Conserve energy, reduce air pollution, avoid toxic materials, maximize recycling – these four principles guided Randolph Croxton and Kirsten Childs, of the Croxton Collaborative, in their "full spectrum" environmental office retrofit for the National Audubon Society, New York. Housed in a fine old Manhattan building, it has conserved this while saving enormously on resources by avoiding new building. The spirit of the Audubon Society's work is captured in the new etched glass conference room doors.*

RIGHT: *Bill McDonough's retrofit for the Environmental Defense Fund, completed in 1986, was one of the first in the US to create a healthy and ecologically sound working environment. "We avoided carpet glues and formaldehyde, and tacked down the carpet. We looked to avoid waste during construction, and looked for building materials packed in recycled cardboard." The offices are light, airy, and colourful with work places grouped along the "boulevard" lined with ficus trees and street lamps (SEE ALSO P.13).*

Arthur Dyson's professional training is grounded in the very roots of organic architecture. He first started as an apprentice to Frank Lloyd Wright, then worked for Bruce Goff. Later, he returned to his native California to work for William Gray Purcell of the revered Purcell & Elmslie partnership – George Grant Elmslie having been the former chief draughtsman to Louis Sullivan.

Since he set up practice in Fresno in 1969, he has produced a cascade of novel and sophisticated designs. He prefers to describe his work as "reflexive" rather than "organic" as its focus is to try to understand and express the flux of life and its myriad relationships. According to Dyson, the resulting architecture is not only practical in terms of economy and environment, but possesses the vital spark of originality that integrates and exalts the worth of the individual within the surging field of life. The building is an interactive membrane between the dynamic forces seeking expression from within and those coming from outside.

One of his most successful designs for a private house is the Lencioni Residence (LEFT), completed in 1986 and situated in a forested glade in Sanger, California. It was the rhythm of the site together with the adventurous ideas of the young clients that helped Dyson to create the design's dramatic sinuous and fluid forms.

Not only should we aim to reduce water pollution, but also enhance water's curative and life-supporting functions. Water "flow forms" are one of the most effective and beautiful ways of achieving this. Developed by sculptor John Wilkes, the rhythmical flows help oxygenation and are of benefit to water life.

ONE

ANCESTRAL ARCHETYPES

In the span of time it is only yesterday that the Western world departed from ancient tradition. For thousands of years, our ancestors in many different cultures had shared a similar view of their relation to the cosmos, the earth, and their fellow creatures. It was a world view that saw humanity, not as the master race conquering nature for its own ends, but as a co-habitant of this beautiful and unique place in the universe. This being so, our forebears respected and honoured the primeval forces – earth, air, fire, and water – that shaped their world, always seeking harmony with them. Perhaps more important, they also sought to harmonize their inner world of cultural beliefs with the spiritual forces they perceived surrounding them, to secure their place in this world and the world beyond.

The dawning of the modern age – the so-called "Age of Reason" of Descartes – with its rational, scientific disciplines, established religions, and industrial transformation, radically upturned this ancient, almost unbroken paradigm of the world. This paradigm deeply pervaded every part of early peoples' existence – from birth to maturity and eventual death, reaching into the afterlife and even on into reincarnation. Daily routines, seasonal cycles, and annual rituals were all dedicated to this world view. The basics of life – food and shelter – were strands of this giant web. Shelter, whether for the living or the dead, was imbued with symbolism. This symbolism, linking the physical artefact with the spiritual world, found expression in archetypal forms of building in almost every culture. These primordial models embodied the cosmic order, encapsulated the teachings of the gods, and were daily reminders for proper ritual practice. Despite their enormous range and diversity, worldwide they expressed that same broad paradigm.

Most important was shelter for the dead. Throughout Europe and the Americas, burial sites became an integral part of what archaeologists term "ritual landscapes" that linked individual sites and manipulated the spaces between them. Four thousand years ago in Neolithic England, for example, a series of monumental works existed covering vast areas of the countryside. One such monument, the "Dorset Cursus", was a huge swathe of land enclosed by two parallel lines of gleaming white chalk more than 6 miles (10 kilometres) long, probably looking much like a modern freeway. It has been estimated that it may have taken 10 million hours of labour in its construction. The "Cursus" connected several *long barrows* and directed the eye toward skyline burial mounds where the sun set at the equinox. Functioning possibly as a sacred path for the journey of the dead to their last point on earth, it established a timeless link between the ancestors and the natural world. Major ritual sites, such as Stonehenge, were not just single monuments, they were part of a greater order and were connected by a web of landscape features – natural and artificial – to others beyond. At a time when the land was still largely covered by ancient forests, these human constructs must have made a remarkable impact on the mind and spirit of these early peoples.

In many early cultures, homes for the living were also resting places for the dead. In the 9000-year-old Anatolian city of Çatal Hüyük, Turkey, the closely packed houses had rooms that were shrines to the cult of the long-horned bull. Excavation below the floors of living and sleeping areas unearthed skeletons of earlier residents thought to be family ancestors. While the more formal ceremonies were led by priests and priestesses in the main sacred centres, the home was the focus for family worship. In the city of Ur, Mesopotamia, the mud-brick courtyard houses invariably had within them a small family tomb and shrine.

Even when the dead were not housed with the living, deep spiritual elements were maintained in the home. In Egypt, small statuettes to household deities were worshipped. A favourite god, Bes, part lion and part dwarf, often held a sword to protect the family in this life and the next. For the ancient Greeks, keeping the home fire burning honoured Hestia, the goddess of the hearth, and offerings by the head of the family at the altars of family gods and goddesses were all part of the daily routine.

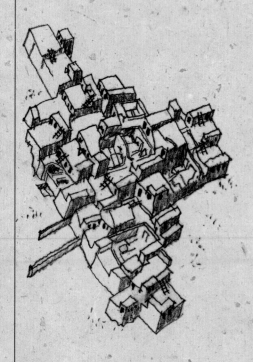

Artist's reconstruction of Çatal Hüyük, Turkey.

In Asia, nomadic peoples transported their spiritual world with them and their portable homes provided other great archetypal expressions of the earth-to-spirit link (as they still do today over much of central Asia). The central Asian steppe stretches from the Caspian Sea, through southern Russia and northern China, to Mongolia and Siberia. Living in this vast land of severe winters, high winds, and sparse rainfall are the nomadic tribes descended from the great Mongol hordes. For 3000 years these tribes have lived in portable dwellings which the Turkic-speaking peoples call yurts. Their circular form and dome-like roofs are extremely strong and stable allowing them to withstand months of heavy gales. Layers (sometimes up to eight) of felt matting laid over the willow lattice frame and roof poles insulate the interior even from the severest cold.

The spatial arrangement inside a yurt has many similarities to that of a North American hogan (SEE P.33). The entrance faces east or southwest depending on the tribe. Inside, the circular space is divided into four quadrants and everyone and everything has its appointed place. There is a women's side and a men's side with a "place of honour" near the altar behind the hearth away from the cold. The herders and newborn animals are near the door. Saddles, guns, and ropes are placed on the men's side; while churn, kitchen tools, and cradle are on the women's side. The earth floor, wooden hearth square, iron tripod, and kettle of water placed over the fire symbolize the Eastern elements of earth, wood, metal, water, and fire. The roof symbolizes the sky and the open smoke hole is the "Eye of Heaven".

"…the silk-fine felt white as a shell
Whiter than snow stronger than bone
Put this way and that on the pure
white roof
The floss-white felt covering a
thousand tents
May you all who use it live in Peace
In the middle of the fair Plain
In your round White Palaces…"

MONGOLIAN FELTING CHANT

Yurts in the central Asian steppe.

Another very ancient archetype is found among the Australian aborigines. Although they don't have permanent shelters they have an intricate spiritual map of their landscape based around ancestral paths and "dreamtime" wanderings. The earth-to-spirit link is so strong that if removed from their ancestral homelands they become sick, as do the bush people of Africa.

In the New World, the ancient paradigm followed its own path among the ritual landscapes of the Amerindian peoples. The yurt found its parallel in the tipi, the hogan, and various similar structures. More than a home, the tipi was a spiritual shelter. To ensure protection and a propitious future for a household and their "lodge" or home, direction and blessing had to be sought from the sacred spirits. Transported by fasting and prayer, the vision seeker would enter the spirit world. A "guardian spirit" would appear as a supernatural animal or bird – the Eagle and mythical Thunderbird being the most powerful guardians to receive. The spirit would then give the visionary instruction on household sacred objects, house-blessing songs, and the symbolic painting of the vision of the world to appear on the tipi cover. The painting usually occupied the spirit-world space, the middle area of the tipi cover, between the dark bands of earth at the base and sky at the peak.

Among the settled Indians other parallels with the Old World emerged. Like Mesopotamian temple mounds or Egyptian pyramids, the sacred buildings of the Central and South American Indians reached for the sky. Mayan temples, for example, such as Tikal, soared to awesome height above the tropical rainforest canopy and formed part of a complex and extensive sacred landscape.

Mayan temples rise above the forest, Tikal, Guatemala.

One of the oldest and simplest archetypes, shared by the Old and New Worlds, is the pit house. This was the predominant Neolithic form of Europe and the Near East. The spiritual significance of these Old World structures is little understood; their history is now visible only in the archaeological traces of post holes and hearths. But in the New World, more is recorded about pit-house cultures since the houses were inhabited until comparatively recently. A well-studied example is the pit-house culture of the Plateau region, the area covering southern British Columbia, Washington state, and parts of Oregon and Idaho. This culture reached its peak around the 13th century but was still in evidence at the end of the 19th. As Peter Nabakov and Robert Easton recount in their excellent book, *Native American Architecture*:

Plateau Indian pit house with notched log ladder.

> "*They* [the Thompson tribe of British Columbia circa 1890] *described their concept of the world as a huge, circular lodge divided into four compartments, each associated with one of the four cardinal directions. This pattern is reflected in the spatial arrangement of their old pit houses, which were divided by four roof beams. They believed that after death one's soul left the world and crossed a river to the east where it resided in the land of ghosts ... To the Thompson, as to many Indian people, it seemed natural to envision their cosmology in architectural terms.*"

The notched-log entry ladder, which usually rested against the eastern edge of the smoke hole, often had a carved bird or animal head painted to represent the guardian spirit of the household.

Another classic archetype, the pueblo, was created by the Pueblo Indians in the southwestern states – the Hopi, Zuni, and Tewa-speaking peoples. The pueblo reaches back to the peoples the Navajo called Anasazi or "Ancient Ones". These people were semi-nomadic hunters and gatherers who, in the first few centuries BC, started to form villages and cultivate maize, beans, and squash. Between 700 and 200 BC, early Anasazi, known as the Basket-makers (owing to their pre-pottery use of finely woven baskets), inhabited caves and earth-covered pit houses. After this, as they became settled, they began to build above-ground villages known as pueblos, which consisted of clustered earth-built dwellings and storage rooms entered from the roof. They also used the pit-house prototype to create semi-underground ceremonial chambers (kivas) within the pueblo. At their zenith, around the 12th and 13th centuries, the Anasazi constructed very large pueblos – multi-roomed, multi-level structures such as those at Chaco Canyon, Canyon de Chelly, and around Mesa Verde. (Although not related, these pueblos show an interesting similarity to the compact cellular units of those much earlier prototypes at Çatal Hüyük!)

By the mid-1100s the inhabitants had begun to abandon the Four Corners area (where Utah, Colorado, Arizona, and New Mexico meet), although why is not known. Prolonged drought, diminishing local resources, and even disease may have contributed to migrations to the Rio Grande valley, the Zuni mountains, the Hopi Mesas, and elsewhere. Although much depleted, first by the Spanish colonization and later by settlers, the pueblo archetype survives today in the inhabited Hopi pueblos and those at Acoma and Taos, New Mexico (SEE PP.100 AND 114).

To the Pueblo Indians, the link of earth to spirit was fundamental to their existence. They believed that their ancestors first lived in a world below the surface of the earth and that they travelled upward through the second and third "planes" to reach the "fourth plane" where humans existed. Above all, lay the domain of the powerful, life-sustaining spirits of sun and rain.

The kiva was the purest archetype for the Pueblo Indians as it symbolically represented the way they emerged from their ancestral underworld home. The kiva, entered by a ladder from the roof, had a ventilation shaft with damper, fire pit, altar, raised platform, wall niche, and a hole in the floor – the sipapu. To the Pueblo Indians the sipapu symbolized the place of emergence – the channel through which the living communicated with the spirits of the dead. It also represented the navel of the earth. The kiva had further significance, symbolizing the four worlds of emergence: the sipapu was the first world, the place of origin; the main floor was the second world, where animals were created; and the end platform was the third world on which rested the access ladder leading out of the top hatchway into the fourth world, the world of the living.

The kiva was also a home for the gods (kachinas), and at annual festivals male members, dressed as kachinas, still re-enact the dance their ancestors performed when they emerged into the beauty of the fourth world. Some kivas had wall paintings of tribal kachinas. The kiva may also have represented the wider world of the Pueblo Indians. The four roof beams were the first four trees on earth, the roof was the Milky Way, the walls were "the sky", and hollows in the walls were the four sacred mountains at the cardinal points protecting the pueblo lands.

> "Now comes the dawn,
> The universe grows green,
> The road to the Underworld
> Is open! Yet now we live,
> Upward going, upward going!"

Songs of the Tewa translated by Herbert J Spinden.

Interior of Hopi rectangular kiva.

The belief that buildings on the earth are models for the relationship between people and the spirit world is shared by the Dineh, the "People", or the Navajo, as they are now generally known. According to their creation myth, "Blessingway", the first man and woman emerged through three underworlds to be met by Talking God. The God proceeded to make them their first "home places" or hogans – a "male" hogan and "female" hogan fashioned after two sacred mountains in New Mexico (these were referred to respectively as the "heart of the earth" and "lungs of the earth"). Talking God decreed that the hogan entrance face east toward the rising sun, the main support poles (representing Mountain, Water, Corn, and Earth worlds) be located toward the four cardinal points (north, south, east, and west), and under each post, pieces of the sacred "jewels" of white shell, turquoise, abalone, and obsidian (of which the mythic prototype posts were made) be placed as a symbolic linking to the primordial hogan. Anyone entering a hogan must take a sunwise direction around the central fireplace, passing the male/day side (south) and the seat of honour (west), to come to the female/night side (north). Even though today they represent only a few of the buildings of a modern Navajo compound, hogans are still built, lived in, and used for tribal ceremonies.

Navajo hogan (female) with earth-covered roof.

All across the world in hugely diverse cultures there are examples in early building of this close intertwining of the spirit world with that of the earthly life. But, as time progressed, the two became increasingly separated. No doubt at the heart of this parting of the ways was the fundamental change in each society from "pagan" or "animist" world views to the worship of one deity. This change was later reinforced by the rise of secular power and the rationalized world view. Gradually, the ancient archetypes declined or were subsumed by Christianity and other major religions. Churches, temples, and mosques were built over pagan sites and homes became secularized.

Nonetheless, the archetypes are still alive in many parts of the world. Some, such as the yurt and the kiva, have survived, while others, such as the tipi and underground house, are being revived. Echoes of spiritual meaning are found in many homes whether in superstition or in religious observance and there are still places where the ancient paradigm persists today. Indeed, in many parts of the world, indigenous peoples are even prepared to fight to restore their ancestral culture.

In a world that has grown rational and cold and has lost much of its meaning, architects and designers, like other people, are looking back to ancient archetypes for new direction and inspiration. One of these is Keith Critchlow who has spent the best part of his life studying what he calls "sacred geometry". Drawing on Eastern and

Western art, science, and philosophy, he seeks to demonstrate the fundamental power of geometry to place us in harmony with the environment and ourselves. Applying the laws of geometry to proportion, he searches for an eternal balance in his designs, so that like those of their forebears, they have about them a timeless and classical quality. He conceived the basic idea for his design of the Krishnamurti Centre, England, as a person seated cross-legged looking at the view. This image expressed for him the central theme of the building as "The world is you, and you are the world." A "quiet room" and peaceful courtyard act as the focus, while the "legs" of the sitting person become the accommodation wings. The simple design is filled with light; its spaces and forms have a natural resonance with the older buildings of Thoronet Abbey nearby, and the whole design bears out one of Critchlow's favourite sayings, that of philosopher S H Nasr: "There is nothing more timely than the timeless."

Another example of the survival of an ancestral paradigm is to be found in Hong Kong where the ancient Chinese art of placement, *feng shui*, is still being applied to modern buildings. Architects and building owners there usually employ a feng shui expert to ensure that the design of new buildings will be as harmonious and propitious as possible for the occupants.

A lesser-known example is the modern adaptation of the ancient Hindu Sanskrit writings, the *Vedas*, termed *Sthapatya-Ved*, meaning literally "to establish knowledge". Under the auspices of Maharishi Mahesh Yogi, well known for his Transcendental Meditation institutes, this Vedic knowledge is now being applied to architecture and other art and design disciplines. According to the Maharishi, *Sthapatya-Ved* gives guidance for organizing the environment in ways that promote perfect health, prosperity, and the evolution of the individual, society, and the environment as a whole. Using what is called "Natural Law" (the laws that govern nature) and the three main principles – Right Direction, Right Proportion, and Right Placement – the Maharishi and his followers believe that their emerging plans for cities for 100–200 families on every continent will produce "ideal communities with amenities for natural health care, ideal education, harmonious community life and the opportunity for each individual to grow in the full dignity of inner life."

*Monumental burial mounds were constructed across much
of present-day Europe during the Neolithic Age. One of the
finest restored examples in England is the Belas Knap long
barrow in Gloucestershire dating from about 2500 BC. Its
long earth mound has "false entrances" leading nowhere.
The real stone chambers (ABOVE) are entered from the sides.*

To the Miwok, the California Valley oak was not merely a source of acorn flour – their staple food – it was also sacred. Their villages encircled a large oak which symbolized the centre of the world. The traditional Miwok homes, called u'macha (BELOW), were built of pine and cedar poles tied with wild grape vines or willow (SEE P.38) and covered with incense-rich cedar bark taken from dead trees.

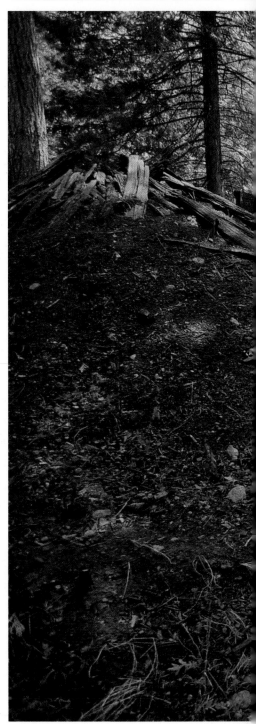

One of the earlier reconstructions of the roundhouse is found in the Indian village in Yosemite National Park (RIGHT). The village recreates Miwok culture of the 1870s, 20 years after initial contact with non-Indians. Like their homes, the roundhouse roof was covered with incense-rich cedar bark. The smaller building in the background is the sweathouse, used for ceremonial purification before dancing and hunting.

The Miwok home had a framework of pine and cedar poles (SEE P.36).

In the turbulent times of the first millennium BC, *Celtic settlements were protected by formidable defences. Always strategically located on hilltops and spurs, they were also surrounded by "ringworks" of strong wooden palisades with towers, steep earth mounds, and ditches. The hillfort at Castell Henllys, Dyfed, Wales* (ABOVE), *was probably occupied during the Iron Age about 250* BC. *The reconstructed roundhouses inside the fort are 33 feet (10 metres) in diameter and have a timber-pole frame thatched with reeds cut from the nearby estuary. The walls* (RIGHT) *are "wattle and daub" – intertwined hazel or willow branches plastered with a mixture of mud, horse hair, and cow dung.*

A semi-underground kiva is situated in a dramatic natural cave 140 feet (43 metres) above the floor of the Frijoles Canyon in Bandelier National Monument, New Mexico. The Anasazi probably settled in the canyon around the late 1100s, attracted by the permanent stream. A pueblo village used to contain many kivas, each built for one of the various family clans that made up the tribe. Primarily used for religious ceremonies, the kiva also served as a place of education for boys and young men. Without a written language, knowledge was passed down orally from one generation to the next via legends, stories, prayers, and songs. Today, kivas are still used by many Pueblo Indians to celebrate their traditional festivals.

Around the 14th century many
Anasazi groups migrated west to
settle beside the Rio Grande. The
ruins of the Kuaua Pueblo in the
Coronado State Monument, New
Mexico, overlook the river. One of
the kivas, when excavated, was found
to have many layers of mural
paintings depicting various kachinas.
The originals, which represent one of
the most important finds of
prehistoric mural painting in North
America, are preserved in the on-site
museum. They are reproduced in the
reconstructed kiva (ABOVE) together
with fire pit, altar, and air vent
(RIGHT). The Pueblo Indians believed
that, as they entered down the ladder
(FAR RIGHT), they were purified by the
smoke of the fire beneath.

Over a million years ago two violent eruptions of the Jemez Volcano covered much of New Mexico, Arizona, and Colorado with 1000 feet (305 metres) of volcanic deposits. Over time, the elements cut deep canyons into the plateau creating isolated "mesas" and gouged many holes within the soft "tuff" rock of the canyon cliffs. Using wood and stone tools, the Anasazi enlarged those on the sunward side to make their early cave dwellings, often reached by ladder (ABOVE and FAR RIGHT). Most caves once had a small flat-roofed room built in front of them. These homes offered good defensive sites, commanding spectacular views, as does the one at Tsankawi, New Mexico (RIGHT), with its panorama of the mesas and the distant Sangre de Cristo Mountains.

The central crown at the top of a yurt is known as the "Eye of Heaven". It is the most difficult part to make as skill in bending wood is needed. Across the crown are fastened wooden rods bent in a concave curve to hold up the smoke flap. Each tribe has its own pattern for these rods; and from inside the yurt they make a striking configuration against the sky. The example (BELOW) is from a yurt modelled on those of the Turkoman tribe, made by Hal Wynne-Jones, an Englishman trained in Turkey, who is promoting yurts as shelters for the homeless and refugees.

"You have noticed that everything an Indian does is in a circle, and that is because the Power of the World is in a circle, and everything tries to be round ... Even the seasons form a great circle in their changing, and always come back to where they were. The life of a man is a circle from childhood to childhood and so it is in everything where power moves. Our tipis were round like the nests of birds and these were always in a circle, the nations hoop, a nest of many nests where the Great Spirit meant for us to hatch our children."

Autobiography of Hehaka Sapa (Black Elk), Oglala Sioux/Lakota holyman.

"Visitors exclaim over the beautiful light in the tipi. During the day it is cheerful and mellow . . . Even on dark, gloomy days it is brighter than most houses. But especially the nights are wonderful . . . some nights the moon climbs right up over the poles and looks in. Outside a coyote howls or a great horned owl hoots in the distance."

The Indian Tipi by Reginald and Gladys Laubin.

"Today is the day I put up my home. I leave you to the care of the four winds ... You, our Maker, direct us whether it be good or bad; it is your will. Help us to think of you every day we live in this lodge; guard us in our sleep; wake us in the morning with clean minds for the day, and keep harm from us."

Dedication of a Plains Cree tipi.

TWO

HEALING ARCHITECTURE

"Buildings, too, are the children of Earth and Sun"
FRANK LLOYD WRIGHT

A ccording to the ancient
cultural paradigms of early peoples, and many indigenous peoples today, it is impossible to separate the health and wellbeing of the body from that of the spirit. In oriental medicine, for example, it is believed that you become sick, not so much from an infection, but more from an imbalance in your life. The underlying philosophy of oriental medicine is based on the restoration of balance and harmony in the whole person. Not so with conventional Western medicine and science. Both have diverged from such classic traditions, even though scientist philosophers such as Fritjof Capra, Rupert Sheldrake, and James Lovelock have amply shown how the current mechanistic world view and disconnected specialisms of modern science are both outmoded and destructive. Orthodox medicine suffers from the same defects, although fortunately there is now a move toward a new healing approach in the West.

In architecture, this new awareness can be witnessed in Europe, especially in Germanic countries and Scandinavia, via the growth over the last decade of the *Baubiologie* or Building Biology movement. This combines healthy building with an ecological and spiritual sensitivity. In North America, a similar shift is taking place. Inspired by a desire to combat chemical pollution and toxic environments, pioneers such as Debra Dadd-Redalia have long campaigned for modern lifestyles that are "non-toxic, natural and earth-wise". The US architect/builder Paul Bierman-Lytle now has many healthy buildings to his credit and a successful "outfitters" marketing environmentally sound construction supplies.

More recently, John Bower, author of *The Healthy House*, has done much to promote the "healthy home". There is also a move toward the more fundamental concept of "healing environments" – a concept that, for Carol Venolia, West Coast architect and author, connects bodily health with a deeper spiritual wellbeing.

"When you are in a healing environment, you know it; no analysis is required. You somehow feel welcome, balanced, and at one with yourself and the world. You are relaxed and stimulated, reassured ... you feel at home."

CAROL VENOLIA

One of the most interesting and deeply philosophical strands of healing design is organic architecture. Although often attributed to Frank Lloyd Wright (1869–1959), the movement really stemmed from the Pre-Raphaelites, the Arts and Crafts Movement, and Art Nouveau (or Jurgendstil) in Europe. The American organic vernacular was probably initiated in the 1870s by H H Richardson who, by re-interpreting the symbolism and geometry of Romanesque and Gothic styles, produced a range of remarkable churches and libraries around Boston. Influenced by him, Louis Sullivan began to use florid vegetative "organic" designs to decorate his functional austere buildings, such as the Auditorium Building in Chicago. Meanwhile in Brussels, Victor Horta used flowing tendril motifs to embellish his houses. Wright, who had studied and worked with Sullivan, immediately took the organic element and developed it in his own work as a major theme.

With Wright organic design was not just decoration or style, it became the underlying inspiration. He wanted his buildings to be intimate with nature and literally to love the ground on which they stood. He felt the ground to be more important than the building, for the ground would endure the longer, and was very much in sympathy with Thoreau's view that we are, "but a sojourner in nature". Because nature is not symmetrical, Wright felt the same should be true of a building if it was to reflect the organic and the living. He preferred a dynamic balance of forms and spaces, and enjoyed creating a sense of delight and surprise. Hence, in Wright's buildings, you could walk from a closed and restricted space, to one which was light, open, and airy – as if you had emerged from a dark forest into a sunny meadow.

Another powerful influence that helped organic architecture to establish itself was Rudolf Steiner (1861–1925), the founder of *anthroposophy*. His writings and teachings drew on the philosophy of Goethe, who believed that it was primarily through our bodily movements that we experience architecture. Moving through a building can be a pleasurable experience, similar to dancing. A fundamental tenet of anthroposophic organic architecture is that form has a profound effect on behaviour and feelings. Steiner proposed, for example, that it was the Gothic cathedral that caused the mystical character of the Middle Ages, and not the reverse.

Today anthroposophic architects contend that organic buildings will help their inhabitants to feel, not only a sense of wellbeing, but a new creativity and individuality coming into their lives and work. They believe that rectangular buildings, or those built like cubes, cause people to think and act in a predominantly rational, coldly logical, materialistic (and probably masculine) way – to make what the Dutch architect Ton Alberts calls "cube-world". Alberts, who

Staircase at 6 rue Paul-Émile Janson, Brussels, by Victor Horta, 1893.

won the commission to design the headquarters of the bank of the International Netherlands Group (ING) in Amsterdam, is inspired by the possibilities of a different architecture, using a diversity of angles. He maintains that walls built with love contain a certain aura, whereas walls built by machines are cold and rational, yielding nothing. A building that is constructed from the heart will always evoke love in the people that come into contact with it. Indeed, the ING Bank building is a remarkable testament to his philosophy. Not only is it ecologically designed, making it extremely energy-efficient, but it is also a beautiful place. Its real contribution to the new architecture, however, is its facility to make its occupants, and its 120,000 visitors a year, feel rejuvenated, positive, and at ease – a truly healing environment.

There are now many examples of anthroposophic organic architecture around the world. In Wales, for instance, Christopher Day has created many low-cost self-build projects such as a Steiner kindergarten, a retreat, and stone-built turf-roofed houses. In North America and Europe, many local examples of Steiner and Waldorf schools and nurseries show features of anthroposophic design, especially in the use of colour, materials, and asymmetrical flowing forms. In Sweden, the Rudolf Steiner Seminariet, Järna, is one of the most fully developed and now has a stimulating range of buildings, mostly the work of Erik Asmussen. He has his design studio there, lives in a house he designed, and has been a part of the community for many years. The Seminariet has a number of *husets* or houses such as those for *eurythmy* dance and music which combine teaching spaces with halls at the top and living accommodation below; others are the student hostels, library, dining room, and shop plus the Vidarclinic, Orjan School, and the most recent, the Great Hall. The beautiful site also has extensive gardens, a biodynamic market garden, and biological ponds.

The buildings and settings subtly express a dynamic equilibrium between opposites. Spatially, like a dance, you feel a sense of rest-in-movement and movement-in-rest. Symmetrical forms contrast, yet are balanced, with asymmetrical ones; low sheltered intimate spaces interplay with high open communal areas; warm expansive reds, yellows, and ochres interact with cool contracting blues, violets, and greys. The contained massing of the tall blue *husets*, for example, contrasts and balances with the low extended serpentine form of the orange-rose Ormen Lange (student apartments); the rounded roofs of the Robygge (red houses) complement the angular lines of the Almandinen (blue houses). Even the details display this. In one communal hall, each wall has a window of a special shape and size to express the particular qualities of natural light coming from north, south, east, and west (SEE P.57).

Organic facade of ING Bank, Amsterdam.

"*Every angle has its own angel. There is ninety degrees which has an angel. But between zero and ninety degrees there are eighty-nine other degrees, so there are enormous possibilities for calling all kinds of angels to come into our buildings*".

TON ALBERTS

Asmussen also draws on Goethe's and Steiner's concept of metamorphosis. Goethe maintained that you could imagine a whole plant as the metamorphosis of the archetypal "leaf". Seed, bud, leaf, flower, and fruit are all transformations, yet parts of a single organic process. In a similar way, a "living" and "organic" building grows out of the archetypal idea – each form, space, texture, and colour developing this idea and changing it, not only to serve different activities, but above all, to inspire and nourish the whole person. By offering choice, the building's forms help to reinforce the individual – which strengthens the self-healing process.

In Hungary, organic architecture has taken off in quite another direction. Born against the repression of harsh grey concrete cubes and huge slab blocks of socialistic modernism, organic architecture has become a symbol of freedom and renewal of traditional values. The two outstanding figures are Imre Makovecz and Gyorgy Csete. Both were keen to throw off the alien ideology and re-establish Hungarian culture. For Makovecz, Steiner and Wright were starting points. For Csete, inspiration was found in building on the traditions of Hungarian Art Nouveau. Both architects drew on the rich sources of Magyar folk art and vernacular building. Csete's best-known building – the Well-House and Sun Church – appears to hover over the forest floor, its beautiful tulip-shaped head and glass dome rising up from the circular plinth. Seeming at once modern and old, the design recalls both a medieval timber church and futuristic space craft.

Makovecz, now an internationally renowned figure, has many exciting works to his credit. His design language is a complex mix of spirituality and romanticism, with fragments from Hungarian history and myth – nomadic tents, medieval castles and church spires, angels' wings, and domes. His love of natural forms and materials is evident in the use of whole trees, timber whale-like interiors, and the simple folk building language of whitewashed walls, arched verandahs, slate roofs, and tile stoves. Although eclectic, his buildings never lack unity: they are always bold, passionate, and dramatic. He and Csete have taught and inspired a large following of young Hungarian architects, to the extent that organic architecture has almost become *the* national style.

But is organic architecture ecological too? Anthroposophists have usually been more inspired by "human and spiritual ecology" (notably the influence of form, space, and colour on humans), than by today's broader environmental concerns about the welfare of *all* species. Therefore, for a building to be truly organic and ecological it needs to synchronize with a broader perspective. Perhaps we need to act and design more in terms of what Dutch environmentalist Kees Zoeteman has coined as "Gaia-sophy".

Three earth-and-clay houses have been built on anthroposophic principles for the Nibble School at Järna, Sweden. The top floor of the curving three-storey school building is lit by a series of unusual and beautifully shaped windows set in a wall niche framing a view of the forest.

(Prisma Architects, Sweden)

The Great Hall at Järna (ABOVE) is a cultural centre with a large auditorium lit by natural daylight, a foyer (SEE P.56), activity rooms, and housing. "As we understand it," explains the architect Erik Asmussen, "the goal for anthroposophic architecture is, through design and the whole form-language, to strive to create a stimulating environment, which, through its special atmosphere, can act as an inspiration to the activity for which the building is intended."

The Vidarclinic, also designed by Asmussen, is the healing centre at Järna. It comprises a 74-bed hospital, doctors' housing and consulting rooms, and facilities for outpatient care. The essential experience of the clinic derived from its forms, spaces, colours, textures, and scents is one of healing. The environment helps to strengthen the will, believed to be essential to the process of self-healing and rebalancing the individual. The ambulatory (corridor) which gives

views on to the central courtyard (RIGHT) is ever changing. Broadening out for public spaces, closing in for more intimate sitting places, travelling from light to dark, it also creates a journey through colour, both subtle and strong. The spatial flow echoes Steiner's description of his own buildings at Dornach: "The wall is not merely a wall, it is living, just like an organism that allows elevations and depressions to grow out of itself."

The Great Hall at Järna (LEFT) is perhaps the
most beautiful yet of Erik Asmussens's designs;
the foyer displays a maturity and sensitivity in
the interplay of forms and spaces and the
wonderful luminosity created by light, colour,
and reflection. In the large music room at Järna,
the four windows express the character and
quality of their four different orientations. The
largest and most expressive is the south-facing
window (ABOVE).

Every entrance to a building has a unique character, which is thoughtfully expressed in anthroposophic design. The sturdy entrance to the Nibble School at Järna (LEFT), with its bold violet-blue colour, hand-crafted wrought-iron work, and protective canopy, is stimulating and welcoming for children and teachers alike.

(Prisma Architects, Sweden)

The Waldorf School, Stavanger, Norway, was designed by architect Espen Tharaldsen of Arbeidsgruppen HUS in 1989. This major project will take many years to complete. The first classroom wings (ABOVE) were completed with the support of parents (and children) who helped to decorate and finish the interior.

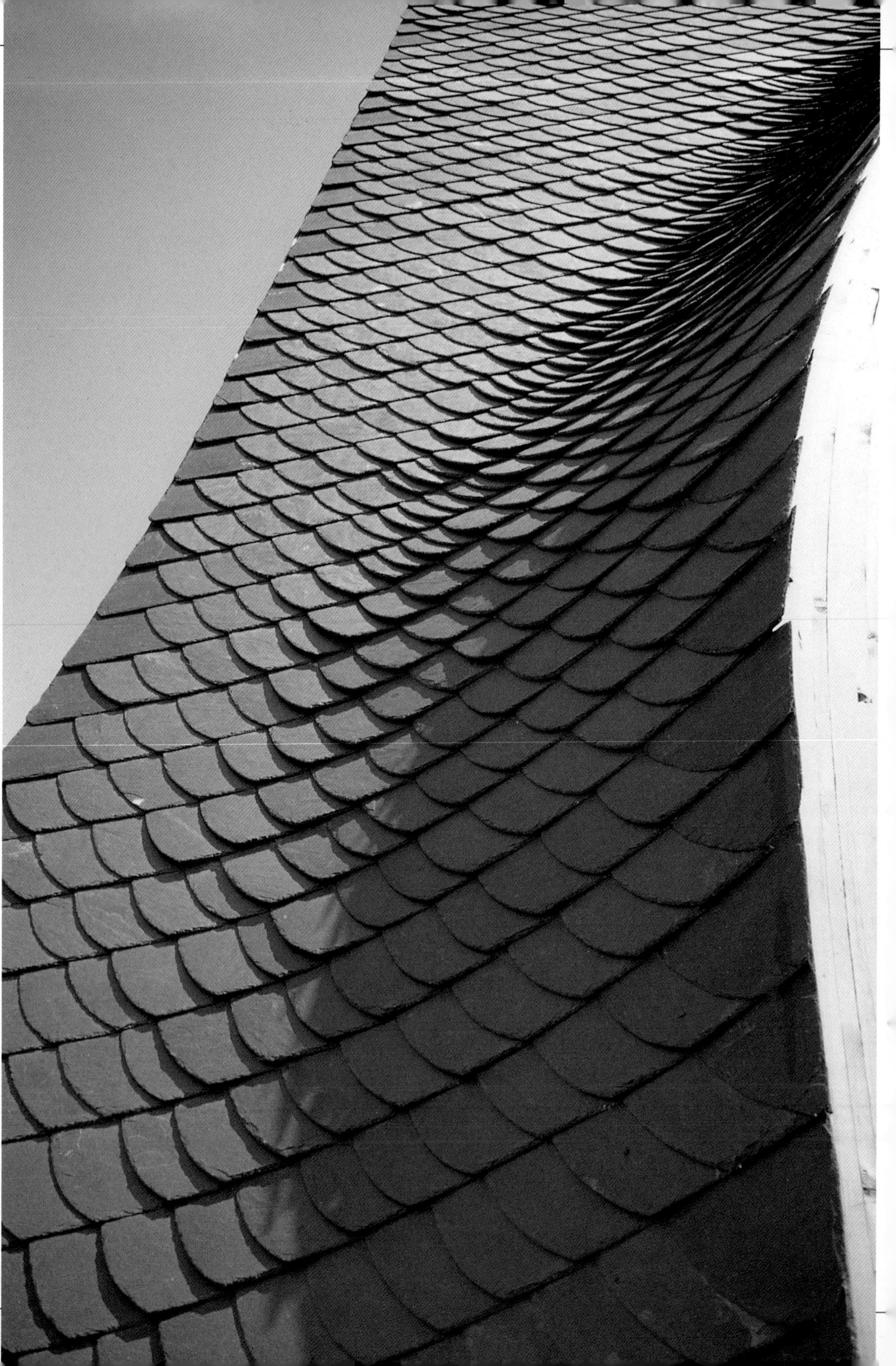

Although originally influenced by the organic architecture of Frank Lloyd Wright and Rudolf Steiner, the organic architecture of Imre Makovecz has a strength and passion borne out of his desire to express Hungarian cultural values. His religious architecture is some of his most inspired, as, for example, the magnificent

Roman Catholic church at Paks (LEFT). The slates seem to sweep over the curving forms of roof and steeple, somewhat reminiscent of the scales of a giant fish! At the Lutheran church at Siófok (ABOVE LEFT) and at Paks (ABOVE RIGHT), German Gothic and Magyar imagery mix to create a unique cultural blend.

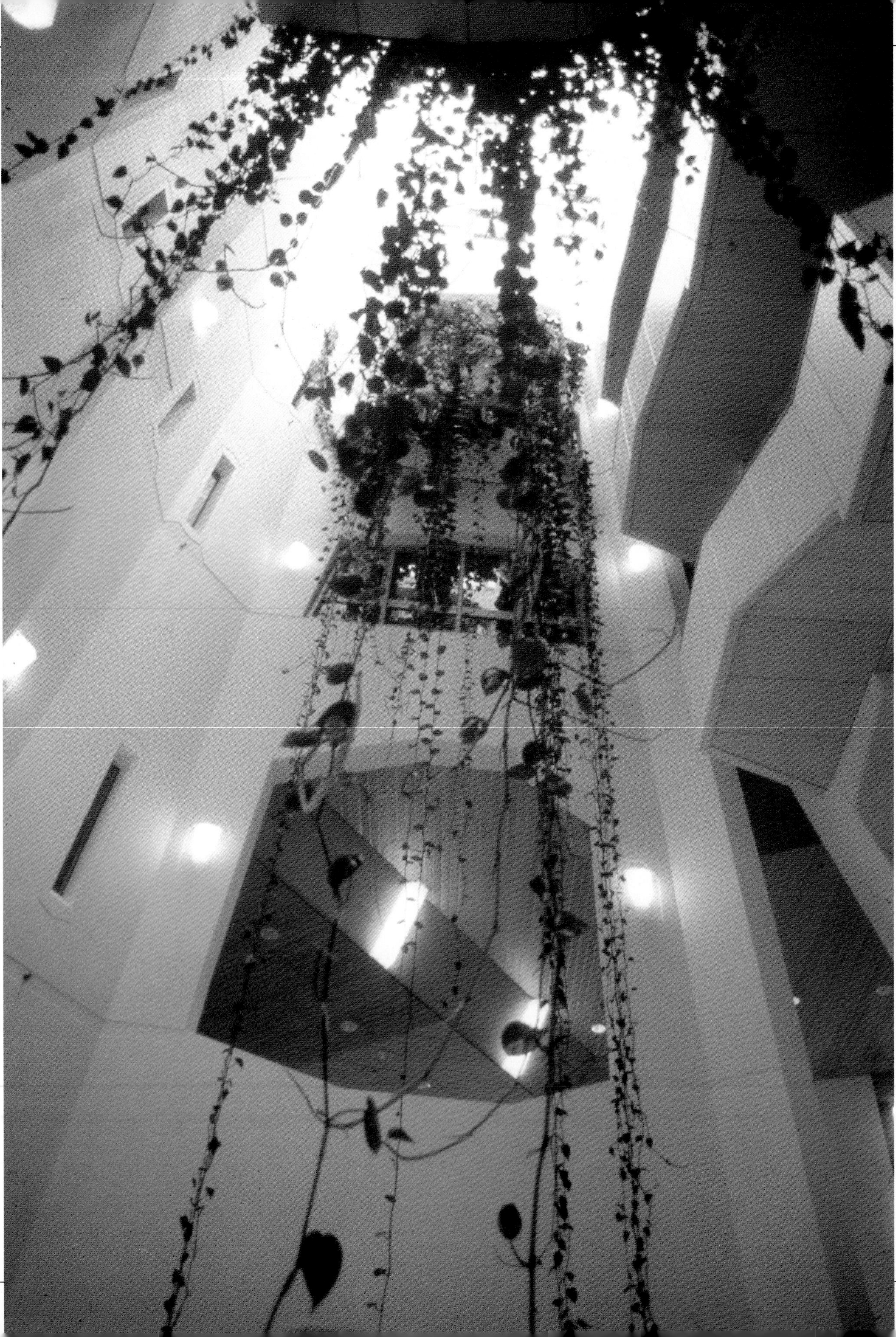

The ING Bank headquarters, Amsterdam, designed by Ton Alberts and M van Huut, is the most ambitious anthroposophic organic architectural project so far. It comprises ten office towers, from three to six storeys high, spaced apart on an irregular S-shape plan. An elevated indoor walkway links them and the restaurants, snack bars, library, auditorium, conference hall, and other facilities sited along its way. Spacious open light wells, at the centre of each tower (LEFT), allow natural daylight to flood into the interior and greenery to cascade down luxuriantly. Rain-water flow forms and sculpture, such as this one (ABOVE), abound along the walkway, bringing sensory pleasure.

"This building is an example of organic and ecological architecture," says Ton Alberts. "I have incorporated the elements of earth, sun, water, air, and space." As the sunlight streams through a striking stained-glass design by Udo Zembok (ABOVE) and water trickles down a sculptured rivulet, the elements are in living harmony. Good interior natural daylight is complemented by the imaginative lighting designs of Theo Crosby of Pentagram Design, London (RIGHT).

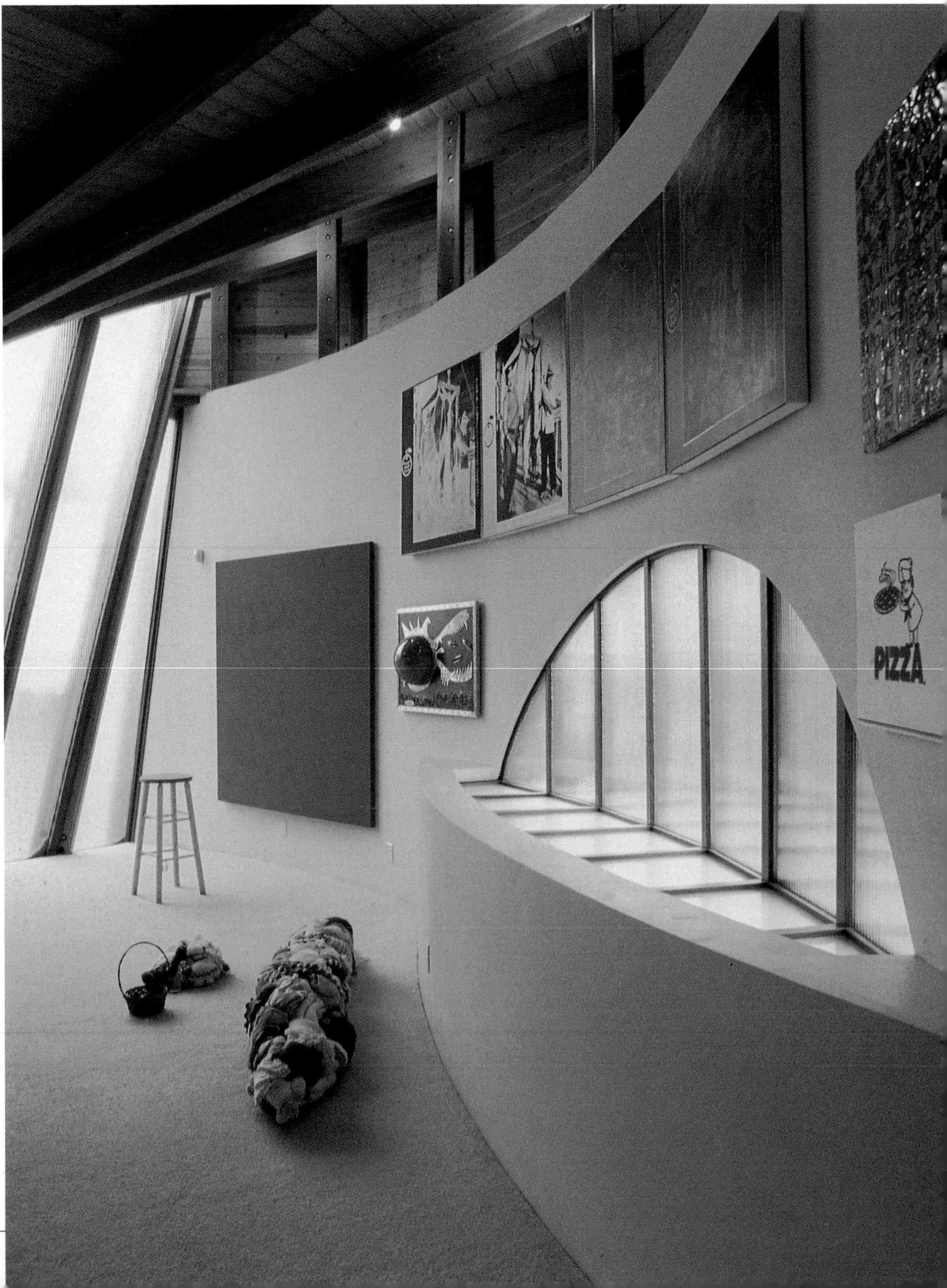
PIZZA

"In 1958 my wife Anne and I began to build our own home in the back of San Diego County. That experience and the long association with Sim Bruce Richards, a San Diego architect who studied with Frank Lloyd Wright in the 1930s, have been crucial in what has developed in my art and building." James Hubbell, painter, sculptor, poet, publisher, and architect, is well known for his many hand-crafted buildings (including the Sea Ranch Chapel) that "exist with nature". Called Ilan-Lael, Hubbell's own residence comprises six separate structures. Shown here are his studio (BELOW) and boys' house (NEAR LEFT) with its vibrant stained-glass bathroom.

LEFT: Although the dramatic free-form designs of Bart Prince are part of an organic tradition stretching from Frank Lloyd Wright to Oklahoman architect Bruce Goff (with whom Wright collaborated), his architecture is really about expressing individuality – that of his clients through his own. The remodelling of the Spence residence, Pasadena, California (1989), included an imaginative "gallery/living room" space (shown here) which, in Prince's words, "stands as a sculptural expression of the lives being lived within by a vital and creative family of individuals."

The Price residence, Corona Del Mar, California (1984–89) is a well-known building by Bart Prince (LEFT). Christopher Mead gives a vivid description in his Houses by Bart Prince:

"Wedged tightly into its site, the Price Residence is shielded from its neighbours to the north and west behind a deeply overhanging, biomorphic roof covered, like the walls, in a rippling, muscular pattern of wood shingles [LEFT] ... Functionally, the Price Residence is conceived as two interpenetrating yet distinct buildings. The upper level ... houses the office of Joe Price and, in three adjacent overlapping pods, his reception and entertainment spaces. The lower, more private and domestic level belongs, following Japanese custom, to Etsuko Price ...

This beautifully crafted house, in whose oceanward foundation is nestled a complete tea house, at once recaptures Frank Lloyd Wright's trans-Pacific dialogue between America and Japan, accepts the heritage of Goff ... and offers a portrait of the owners that could only have been painted by Bart Prince."

The house designed by architect Gernot Minke in Kassel, Germany, is in the form of a series of interlocking octagons. Its log roofs are earth-covered and its walls are earth-sheltered. These, plus the "wintergarden" sunspace, all make for an extremely energy-efficient design. Baubiologie principles prescribed the use of natural materials and organic paints, making it a pleasant and healthy house too. But Minke's main claim to fame is his long-term research, development, and teaching of earth-building techniques at the local university – much of which is used in his work in developing countries.

Here, in the beautiful top-lit entry hall to the house (ABOVE), he has used a novel method for constructing the non-load-bearing internal partition walls. Using clay-earth dug from the site, it is extruded into long sausage shapes which are then slotted into a timber frame. They limit shrinkage cracks to the joints (which are clay-pointed when dry), making for a good internal climate and giving an unusual and interesting surface relief.

THREE

HARMONY WITH THE LAND

Non-industrial societies have little choice but to live in harmony with the land. They can use only local or low-cost materials, energy, and water, and have to be ever aware of their sustainable supply. When "development" occurs, the initial luxury of cheap energy, piped water, and synthetic materials upsets this balance. But once the price becomes apparent in high energy consumption and pollution, environmental awareness reawakens.

The West spawned the first Industrial Revolution, and is now at the forefront in trying to find the way back. For many people, the path to this returning environmental awareness began with practical tasks such as energy conservation and recycling. The oil crisis of the 1970s highlighted the precarious dependence of the Western world on conventional "hard" energy sources, and since that time there has been a drive for greater energy efficiency. This has been boosted of late by fears of global climate change due to rising levels of greenhouse gases in the atmosphere. Although alternative "soft" energy supplies from sun, wind, and water have been promoted, they have rarely received the support they deserve. The small-scale soft energy options have been taken up more readily in non-Western countries where climate conditions are more favourable and public supplies often inadequate. Solar panels, water husbandry, methane gas energy, and wind and water power are now becoming common in large parts of the southern hemisphere, particularly in poorer communities. But in the West, although energy concern is producing an abundance of new environmental projects, from wind farms to huge energy-efficient offices, the soft energy options remain the exception rather than the rule.

Out of these emergent practical steps, people have gradually come to understand that environmental awareness has a broader meaning than merely reducing daily energy, water, and material

Giant electricity generating windmills, Denmark.

consumption. What about the problems created by production? To extract, process, manufacture, and transport the materials needed for building and living uses enormous energy – often called the "embodied energy" of the materials. This wasteful and polluting mode of production, from source to disposal, is typical of the one-way flow of energy and resources which modern industrial societies have come to accept as "normal". Environmental impact studies show the devastating effect these processes can have on the environment. And yet architecture and the design world have only recently begun to reassess building materials and processes in this light, including the value of re-used and recycled materials.

The mainstream environmental concern of governments and professionals responsible for construction today is still focused around energy efficiency. Analagous with the approach of Western medicine, they look at curing the symptoms of disease rather than balancing the whole being. Arne Naess, the Norwegian philosopher and originator of ecosophy (ecological philosophy) differentiates between shallow and deep ecology. Shallow ecology is more concerned with halting pollution and the depletion of world resources. Naess sees this approach as a threat. He believes that it will lead to more growth, a larger gulf between rich and poor, the developed and developing nations, and will favour hard rather than soft technology. Deep ecology, on the other hand, focuses on changing the way people think. Individuality, self-sufficiency, autonomy, creative diversity, and an integrated approach – these are the watchwords of a deeper ecological awareness.

This and other influences such as the *Gaia Theory* of James Lovelock, the more spiritual concerns of Eastern philosophy, and the cultural traditions of ethnic peoples (SEE CHAPTER 5) are the newer sources of thinking. Their ideas have led to a desire for many to find more fundamental ways of living in harmony with the land and rebalancing their relationship with nature; making self-sustaining lifestyles with an emphasis on personal and planetary self-healing and repairing.

One of the keys to this is to see the way we live, and the environment in which we live, as an integral part of an *ecosystem*. To see our habitat not just as somewhere humans live, but a place where we live in partnership with other species – plants, animals, and bacteria. Nature is made up of interwoven ecosystems. Wonderful in their design, they are continuous, interconnected, self-regulating, regenerative, and sustainable. All natural processes which take place within them are part of an ecocycle, in which the waste of one component becomes the raw material of the next; these natural ecocycles are themselves linked into the global cycles of energy, air, and water.

Nature also sustains herself by living off her "income". She not only leaves her "capital" intact (represented by fossil fuel reserves and mineral deposits), but also increases it all the time by laying down some of the carbon captured by photosynthesis. Like an intricate web, everything in the natural world is interrelated – a change in one part can affect the system elsewhere, even far away. According to chaos theory, the initial changes can be very small yet cause a large effect; the vibrations of a butterfly's wing, for example, can cause a chain reaction that may lead eventually to a storm in a rainforest halfway across the world!

The desire for architecture to be in harmony with nature is not merely sentimental or nostalgic, it is a practical necessity if it is to be part of the ecosystem and accord with and be inspired by the same processes. Even though a building is only a temporary and transitory occupier of ecosystem space, it can do a lot of damage while it is there – like a cuckoo, it can take over the nest and live as a parasite. Of course, humans and their shelters *are* part of the ecosystem and have a rightful place there, but within limits. Today these limits have long been exceeded in the developed world – well beyond those of sustainability.

Some people have sought to break the parasitic grip of human settlement on the land through the route of self-sufficiency. Pioneering examples range from the "integral urban house" in Berkeley, California, to Paolo Soleri's visionary desert city of Arcosanti in Arizona. Brenda and Robert Vale's influential book, *The Autonomous House*, has encouraged many to re-examine their lifestyles and the buildings in which they live. More recently, the American frontier spirit has found new expression in attempts to de-link individual homes totally from public energy, water, and sanitation services. As a result, product suppliers are multiplying to serve such independent living.

Paolo Soleri's Arcosanti, Arizona.

One of the most radical forms of de-linking is the "Earthship" concept of architect Mike Reynolds. He believes that buildings, like ships, should be self-contained, independent, and carry the inhabitant to a better future. Buried in earth on three sides, the earthship requires no back-up heating or cooling. Recycled car tyres (earth-filled) make good load-bearing walls and aluminium can "bricks" laid in cement mortar are used for partitions, lightweight arches, and vaults rendered over with mud-plaster. Around 90 earthships have been built so far in New Mexico and Colorado, with plans for public buildings and a futuristic "Wheel Kingdom" in Japan.

Another project, "Ocean Arks and Biospheres", dreamt of by John and Nancy Jack Todd, came to fruition in the New Alchemy Institute, Massachusetts, but the most ambitious de-linking project to date must be Biosphere 2. In this bold venture, a completely enclosed ecosystem has been created within a steel-and-glass structure in the Arizona Desert, near Tucson. Eight "biosphereans" living inside are testing the biosphere's capacity to support human life. The experiment has much to teach us, but we should remember that such artificial systems are not truly independent and cannot solve the wider environmental issues.

The enclosed ecosystems of Biosphere 2, Arizona.

A more fundamental response to the challenge of finding harmony with the land comes from the radical system of farming known as permaculture (from *perma*nent agri*culture*). Originated by the Australians Bill Mollison and David Holmgren, it is based on a philosophy of working with rather than against nature; of designing agriculturally productive ecosystems which mimic the complexity and resilience of natural systems as closely as possible. For many people, permaculture has become more than just a means of growing food; it has broadened into a model for sustainable living at the grass roots level. According to Mollison: "It is the harmonious integration of landscape and people providing their food, energy, shelter, and other material and non-material needs in a sustainable way." From the point of view of architecture and building, permaculture provides a context in which the building is only one of the elements of a whole system. To design a good building you have, first, to get the whole system right.

One of the outstanding instances of this approach comes from the Gaia Group, Norway, who design buildings based totally on ecological principles (SEE ALSO PP.148–9). They have developed the "eco-cycle house" – a house which is designed to be in a constant state of flux with the natural cycles, for the mutual benefit of its human occupants and the local ecosystem. Unlike the conventional design of a modern house, which is essentially linear, consuming natural elements and degrading them to polluted and toxic waste, the eco-cycle house keys into cyclical biological processes. In this way, the outputs from one part of the house become the inputs for another part elsewhere. To ensure that all these aspects are taken into consideration, an agronomist and biologist work alongside the architectural team.

The Gaia Group is an experimental team developing new local low-tech approaches to building. In the eco-cycle house, hygroscopic (moisture-absorbing and -releasing) materials, such as timber, clay products, plaster, and natural plant fibres, help regulate moisture and humidity using their natural properties and cell structures. "Dynamic insulation" in the shell of the building uses the same porous properties to give controlled ventilation through the structure and avoids condensation. Heating and cooling rely on self-regulating thermodynamic forces and reduce to the minimum complicated electrical controls, pumps, and fans. The biological

Gaia Group eco-cycle houses, Oslo and Stavanger, Norway.

processes of plants are used to help refresh the indoor air and to clean and recycle grey water. The construction using robust local materials (mostly earth, wood, and recycled brick) allows simple maintenance and a long life. With all timber components designed to be demountable (glues and mastics avoided in favour of simple joinery details such as metal bolts or wooden pegs), the whole structure and interior are re-usable or recyclable. The house itself is part of a larger permaculture system involving water and waste recycling and cultivation.

Permaculture operates at many levels and beyond the individual house it looks toward whole communities. On a global scale, harmony with the land will ultimately depend on transforming all our human habitats into "ecohabitats". An ecohabitat, on whatever scale, whether an individual building or an entire city, will replicate the natural balance of ecocyclical resource-generating and -degrading processes. It will use rain water and surface water rather than ground water; it will recycle used water and materials rather than use new supplies; re-use old buildings rather than always building new; harness energy from sun, wind, and water rather than fossil fuels; return all nutrients to the soil rather than add artificial fertilizers; and will integrate human needs for food and shelter in harmony with the indigenous ecosystem rather than creating alien and adverse environments. An ecohabitat will also have a sense of place, not only in its orientation to sun and shelter, but in its placement in its surroundings, and in relation to the subtle energies of the ground beneath. Proximity of home, work, schooling, and food production will also encourage local employment and reduce travel.

Many towns and cities have good individual examples of "green" alternatives: Amsterdam's car-free centre; advanced recycling in Milton Keynes, England; and eco-refurbishment of old apartment blocks in Kreuzberg, Berlin. But ecohabitats need to go beyond "greening" to a redesign of the whole system. Fewer successful examples exist of whole communities designed and run on ecohabitat and permaculture lines. Some of the most notable are Danish and North American *co-housing* and Scandinavian and German eco-villages, environmentally aware towns such as Davis, California, and permaculture villages around the world (SEE PP.148–9 AND 154). All these pioneering ventures provide positive examples of how we *can* live in harmony with the land.

Frank Lloyd Wright, one of the masters of modern natural architecture, always attempted to build in harmony with the land. Completed in 1936, Falling Water (ABOVE) is the archetypal expression of Wright's spirit of the land and sense of place. Perched over the Bear Run Waterfall, the building's various cantilevered levels glide over the water like the branches of a tree.

*The beautiful Spanish colonial church of San Jose
in the montane village of Trampas, standing on the
high road between Santa Fe and Taos, New Mexico,
is built in classic adobe style. Its massive earth
walls camber in to support two timber steeples and
an external gallery. Their thickness provides
protection from hot summers and cold snowy winters.
Note the water chutes that cast rain water well
away from the earth walls.*

*In the remodelled kitchen at Penngrove, California,
architect Carol Venolia added arches, a bay window,
skylight, and Spanish-style fireplace. The floor
is tiled and the walls have a three-coat plaster finish
with a natural tint. Solid-wood cabinets, naturally
sealed, have organically shaped fronts and tiled work-
tops. The pendant lamps are made of alabaster
and metal. Off the kitchen is a "California cooler" –
a pantry with screened openings and slatted shelves
for natural cooling.*

Over the last 20 years, architect Mike Reynolds has evolved a method of construction that attempts to restore rather than drain the planet of resources. Called "Earthship", there are now many examples in the US and elsewhere, such as the Habicht Earthship (LEFT) and the Weaver Earthship (ABOVE), near Taos, New Mexico.

The basic structure of Mike Reynolds's earthships consists of load-bearing walls made by pounding earth into used car tyres. These "rubber-encased adobe bricks" are bonded in a similar way to adobe construction. Every room is based on a "U" shaped module of three, 3-feet (0.9-metre) thick, heat-conserving walls. The fourth side faces south and is glazed to provide light and harness the sun's energy. The roof is heavily insulated and covered with earth which is also heaped up over the rear walls. The ideal site is a gentle sun-facing slope allowing the earthship to be "carved" out of the hillside. Inside

partitions are of aluminium cans set in cement and finished with mud-plaster.

A water system heated by solar power or photovoltaics, a rain-water cistern and aeration waterfall, a grey water recycling system, and a solar toilet are all pre-designed to suit people's needs. In addition to three how-to books and hands-on seminars, a New Generic Package containing plans, construction drawings, and details is available from Reynolds's company Solar Survival Architecture to enable you to build your own earthship at minimum cost.

Salt Spring Island is one of many islands in the archipelago off Vancouver Island, British Columbia. It has become home to many innovative and pioneering people. One of these is Bavarian-born Eva Temmel who has created a series of beautiful organic gardens set amid the dense forest of her 15-acre (6-hectare) holding. She learned to garden as a child following the traditional pre-war methods of her father and local farmers of her homeland. Speaking of her land and log home (ABOVE), she says "my house is my harvest". The house is covered with grape vines and inside, large store rooms contain impressive stocks of vegetables, nuts, berries, and fruit (RIGHT), from which she supplies her many relatives, neighbours, and friends.

As well as creating the famous "integral urban house" in Berkeley, California (an environmental showhouse – now closed), the Farallones Institute researched various prototype ecological house designs. Based on Peter Calthorpe's work, Pierre Stephens designed the passive solar cabin (ABOVE) in northern California. Robert Kourik designed the deer-proof and drought-tolerant garden.

The concept of storing heat has a long history, as illustrated by the traditional glazed "eye" tile *szemeskalyha* stove from Hungary (LEFT), and the modern low-emission wood-burning stove, set in a rock surround, from British Columbia, Canada (ABOVE). Properly designed, their heavy construction stores the fire's heat for long periods, gradually releasing a gentle yet solid warmth into the room.

The modern timber house (FAR LEFT), in a stunning location at the top of Mount Maxwell on Salt Spring Island, British Columbia, is virtually autonomous. This is fortunate since it can become completely snow-bound during winter. Heavily insulated and with very low-emissivity glass windows facing south, much of the heating is via passive solar gain. The high-performance wood-burning stove (SEE P.85) provides back-up heat. Electricity is produced via a windmill and photovoltaic cells (NEAR LEFT), while low-energy lights and appliances economize on use.

But new technology is not the preserve of modern houses alone. In the Anaga Hills of northeastern Tenerife lies the troglodyte village of Chinamada (ABOVE). The small houses, hewn out of the volcanic rock of the hillside, may be anything up to 20 square metres (215 square feet) in size and are surprisingly comfortable inside. Recently, photovoltaic panels have been added to provide much-needed electricity.

The Ökohaus, Frankfurt, Germany (ABOVE),
designed by architect Joachim Eble, houses a
printing works, publisher, surgery, offices, and a
women's centre. The core building is enclosed by
greenhouses (LEFT), where planting, water flow
forms, and natural materials create a pleasant
indoor climate. Rain water flushes the toilets and
excess heat from the printing works provides
most of the office heating.

Norwegian farmhouse vernacular has taught the Gaia Group many lessons in building in harmony with the land. At Lista, with the prevailing winds blowing inland off the sea, farm-houses (ABOVE) are oriented end-on to the wind; the barn foremost at the exposed end sheltering the house behind. Farmers discovered that a tree planted at the rear of the house grew into a shape that helped the wind flow past more easily – a precursor to modern aerodynamic design!

For extra shelter from wind and rain, the old way was to cover the exposed end of the barn with a thick matting of juniper bush sprigs, thereby making what is now often called a "sacrificial wall" (LEFT). The members of the Gaia Group, founders of Gaia International (SEE P.148), are also innovative. They have developed an "eco-cycle house" to interact with the natural cycles of the earth in true Gaian style; the house in Stavanger, Norway (RIGHT) with its beautiful staircase, is one of their earlier designs.

The imaginative stone, slate, and timber house at Ahakista, West Cork, Ireland (ABOVE), designed by Paul Leech, an Irish member of Gaia International, is sited in a montane semicircle, on a south-facing peninsula jutting out into the Atlantic. The area has an unusually mild climate due to the Gulf Stream and prevailing southwest winds. The trefoil, or Y-plan of the three-apartment house (one each for the client, her son, and guests), was partly inspired by the local wildflower, the scarlet pimpernel, and maximizes solar gain for the main suite and passively heated sun space. An internal rain-water pool, with underfloor coils and heat pump, helps warm the house in winter and cool it in summer. The stone drum, at the core of the main suite (RIGHT), is a multi-purpose "staff of life", providing structural support, solar store, service duct, and hearth for the living room "den".

OVERLEAF: The pressure for new homes in rural Scotland has led to a proliferation of uninspired "kit homes". Howard Liddell and John Brennan of Gaia Architects in Scotland, however, show how a new home can be self-built and ecologically sound, too. Their project in Tressour Wood, Aberfeldy, winner of "The Daily Telegraph Individual Homes Award", combines vernacular and modern design in harmony with its woodland setting.

At Tressour Wood, Aberfeldy, Scotland, non-toxic soft-wood timber with recycled paper-pulp insulation allows the walls to "breathe", while a two-storey "solar" dormer conservatory requires only supplementary heating from a wood-burning stove and (occasionally) electric radiators. The A-shaped glass wall looks out over the Tay Valley.

FOUR

VERNACULAR WISDOM

Why is our vernacular heritage so important now? The usual reason given is just that it is part of history, part of our heritage. Older buildings are seen as quaint reminders of an age gone forever. But recently there has been a change of emphasis. Vernacular buildings record lifestyles of the past when people had to find a sustainable way of life or perish, just as we will have to now. The new importance of vernacular building is that it has vital ecological lessons for today.

Without the benefit of abundant energy, past communities had to work with their climate. In hot dry climates, for example, buildings were shaded to avoid the unbearable heat of the summer sun by tall vegetation, rock overhangs, or, in flat desert regions, the courtyard building form. Yet they were also oriented to receive the pleasant warmth of the winter sun. Cool prevailing winds were captured by various means, such as the *malqaf* or *badgir* wind scoops of the Middle East. In semi-arid regions, many households had large rain-water storage cisterns, usually underground. Some whole cities, such as Yazd in Iran, even today still rely on a huge network of caverns served by rain, springs, and water brought long distances from the mountains. Massive walls kept buildings cool in summer, as did high ceilings vented at the top to increase air flow.

In colder climates, comfort depended on shelter from prevailing winds by siting, land form, and vegetation, together with low ceilings, thick walls, and few windows on the exposed side. Animals were sheltered in the home for extra warmth. In extreme cold (as in extreme heat), buildings were buried or covered in earth. In wet areas, houses were raised above the ground or had raised floors, with a steep pitched roof and overhanging eaves.

Vernacular building also lacked the benefit of cheap, mass-produced imported materials. It relied, instead, on largely local

Four badgirs *cool an underground reservoir, Yazd, Iran.*

resources and skills. In forested regions, such as Scandinavia, timber building became a fine art, as did earth and brick building in the relatively treeless lands of North Africa and the Near East. Relying on local materials, the colours and forms of vernacular building often harmonized with their settings. Most significant of all, the vernacular building was not, as today, an isolated, single-purpose unit. Most homes were also processing centres for produce and materials needed by the community. Local communities were often largely self-sufficient, creating between themselves all the basic necessities of life.

Much misunderstanding of the past stems from our lack of information; so many indigenous cultures and traditions have disappeared that the link with the knowledge and values formerly passed down from generation to generation has been broken. The demise of vernacular building is part of this general process. All over the world, it is increasingly difficult to find ordinary vernacular buildings in their original form. Even in Britain, with all its planning and preservation controls, more and more traditional houses are being altered and "improved" beyond recognition. Too many come under the curse of the window sales representative: the resulting plastic-coated aluminium or tropical hardwood windows look utterly inappropriate and insensitive to the style and feel of the old house. As for the interior, if not completely gutted, many original features such as doors, built-in dressers, and ranges will inevitably have been ripped out. All too soon, the regional and local distinctiveness is lost, and all houses begin to look the same.

Fortunately, there is a movement emerging in many countries away from "modernization" to "restoration" or "conservation". The building is cherished for its uniqueness, and satisfaction gained from bringing it back to life. The whole process, although not always easy, is a pleasure – the research, the uncovering of original features hidden beneath modern plaster and paint, the salvaging and hunt for replacements, the learning from local inhabitants and craftspeople. There have been many wider approaches, too, to saving the vernacular heritage, ranging from government legislation to historic trusts, covering single buildings or whole "heritage neighbourhoods". Ultimately, however, it is up to the community to see that vernacular buildings have some measure of protection and remain lived in as a part of the modern world.

Museums are a last resort, though at least they preserve some knowledge. The best and most fascinating of these are the "living museums" of which many countries now have examples. As far back as 1870, Artur Hazelius, a Swedish teacher and researcher of Nordic languages, became so concerned at how fast traditional ways were vanishing that he began to collect and rescue cultural objects. Museum displays were not enough for him. He wanted to enhance the historical experience: to show whole houses, furnished traditionally, and with people in them in period costume, together with their farm animals, in a natural landscape. The idea of the first open-air museum was born! In 1891 a large site was found close to the centre of Stockholm called "Skansen" (small fort) and it was to here, over ten hectic years, that buildings from different regions of Sweden were moved, reconstructed, and furnished. Livestock was brought to the farms, and wild areas were provided with the typical wild plants and animals of the natural habitat.

Skansen was intended to be a miniature Sweden both in its buildings and landscape. So, the Skane farmstead from the southernmost Swedish province was sited at the south of the open-air museum surrounded with willows and beeches, while the Delsbo farm, from the northern province of Halsingland, was located to the north of Skansen among birches and pines. In addition to the many farms and cottages, there are now manor houses, summerhouses, churches, schools, workshops, windmills, a small town centre, a Lapp camp, and a Finnish settlement – indeed, a spectrum of Swedish culture between 1500 and the 1920s.

The vision of Hazelius has inspired other countries to follow suit. International folk villages in the 19th-century Paris and Vienna World Exhibitions and Hungary's "ethnographic village" in the 1896 Magyar Exhibition were precursors of today's permanent open-air museums. In Hungary, there are now a number of folk villages, including one, also called Skansen, near to Szentendre in

Farmstead from Kispalád reconstructed at the Skansen Folk Village, Hungary.

the rolling country north of Budapest. More than 300 village and market town buildings from ten regions of Hungary are planned for this 114-acre (46-hectare) site. Two regions have been completed so far with churches, cottages, farmhouses, animal houses, barns, mills, and stores arranged in the pattern of the original towns and villages. As far as possible, even the orientation of the buildings has been maintained.

Although from different regions of Hungary, the single-storey houses shared a remarkably similar layout: room–kitchen– pantry. The central kitchen had generous brick or adobe ovens, often with an open mud-plastered chimney (*kemenyalja*) above to take the smoke from these and the glazed "eye" tile stoves (*szemeskalyha*) in the two adjoining rooms. A diversity of cheap and abundant materials was used – adobe, local timber, thatch, wattle and daub, clay tiles, and slate. It is easy to see how the ethnic forms – simple arched verandahs, whitewashed walls, thatched roofs – have been so powerful an influence on Hungary's modern organic architects such as Makovecz and Csete (SEE P.52).

19th-century Korean manor house re-erected at the Folk Village, South Korea.

South Korea is a fascinating example of a fast-developing country that has suffered many pressures on its traditional culture and vernacular heritage. The ravages of the Korean War, economic and population growth, and the shift away from agricultural to urban living have all taken their toll. In Korea, the village has always been the focus of the traditional way of life and it is this that the Korean Folk Village seeks to preserve. Near to Suwon, south of the capital, Seoul, 250 traditional buildings have been collected from every province in an extensive open-air museum. Farmhouses, mansions, craft workshops, market place, mills, school, and Buddhist temple show rural 19th-century Korean life. The folk village is a working community of ethnic craftspeople: potters, millers, weavers, smiths, mulberry papermakers, and cooks.

The traditional village homes were usually built in L or U shapes with an outer wall to create a courtyard for privacy. They were single-storey with small windows and few doors. Rooms were small too, about 8 feet (2.5 metres) square. A raised wooden verandah outside often linked several rooms and was used for meals in summer. The ancient heating system for a family house, similar to the Roman *hypocaust*, was called ondol or warm floor. Hot smoke from the kitchen stove passed through underfloor ducts, warming the floors of the living rooms before escaping via a chimney at the end of the house. The floor of the ondol room consisted of flagstones covered with clay. On top, a thick layer of oil-paper was waxed to conduct the heat. At night, with the futon-like mattresses laid directly on the floor, the warmth would percolate gently upward to make a more than comfortable bed.

In Sussex, England, The Weald and Downland Open Air Museum was inaugurated in 1967 by a small group of enthusiasts. Their aim was to rescue representative examples of vernacular buildings from the southeast of England, and to increase public awareness of this heritage. Since the museum has space only for a small number of representative buildings, it encourages communities to preserve buildings on their original sites, unless there is no alternative. An informed and sympathetic approach to the preservation and continuing use of these buildings is encouraged, and advice on building conservation is offered directly or via experts. To date, as well as good collections of country crafts and industries, more than 35 historic buildings have been re-erected on the 40-acre (16-hectare) site at Singleton. These include a medieval farmstead with farm livestock, a working water-powered flour mill, a "hands-on" gallery of building materials and techniques, and a 16th-century market hall which is the centrepiece of a growing small town.

The 16th-century Titchfield Market Hall, re-erected at the Weald and Downland Open Air Museum, Sussex, England.

In the New World, preservation programmes have protected some of the most important historic buildings, often located in city centres such as Philadelphia and Boston. The emphasis has been on conserving the heritage of the newcomers to North America – the Mexican, Spanish, and Anglo settlers – and only comparatively recently have there been any attempts to restore and recreate the habitats and lifestyles of the ancient indigenous Indian peoples. As so much has gone, it is usually necessary to create an outdoor museum with reconstructions of the ethnic buildings. Good, well researched examples are becoming more common, such as the Miwok village at the Chaw'se Regional Indian Museum, California (SEE P.36), and the "Plants and People of the Sonoran Desert" exhibit in the Desert Botanical Garden, Papago Park, Phoenix, Arizona. This shows how people lived and used plants during the thousands of years of human occupation of the Sonoran Desert. Six habitats are represented: desert, desert oasis, native crop garden, mesquite bosque (scrub), semi-desert grassland, and chaparral, all with typical human shelters and implements. The shelters were reconstructed by native American Indians and include roundhouses and shade ramadas of the Pima Indians and an Apache wickiup.

But, as excellent and important as these are, they are recreations, not the real thing. Very few examples remain of places where native American Indians have lived traditionally and where they are still living today. Of these, the pueblos of the southwestern states are some of the most remarkable. Perhaps the best-preserved and most famous is Taos Pueblo. Ancient ruins in the Taos Valley indicate that ancestors of the present-day inhabitants lived there nearly a thousand years ago. The main part of the present buildings was probably constructed between AD 1000 and 1450, and appeared much as it does today when the first Spanish explorers arrived in 1540. It is considered to be one of the oldest continuously inhabited communities in the USA.

Today, around 150 people live within the pueblo full-time. Others, who own homes there, live in modern homes outside the pueblo lands, and return to their old homes for tribal ceremonies throughout the year. The Taos Pueblo Indians actively encourage tourism which helps to sustain the pueblo and its spiritual, cultural, and economic health. In 1965, Taos was declared a national historic landmark; in 1970, the sacred Blue Lake and surrounding mountains were returned to pueblo ownership; and in 1987, Taos was nominated to the World Heritage Society as one of the most significant historical cultural landmarks in the world. It is a living witness to the ecology of the pueblo lifestyle.

The Älvros farmstead in the Skansen Open Air Museum,
Stockholm, is a typical traditional northern Swedish farm.
The buildings which come from southeastern Härjedälen
are of timber with weather-proofing birch bark and
wooden plank roofs. The sloping courtyard faces south
and is enclosed by buildings on three sides. Beyond these
stands a 16th-century log cabin with a gallery situated to
the front (ABOVE).

Although the Älvros farmstead had two living rooms, one was the parlour or "best room," only for use on festive occasions. The actual living room (LEFT) had a heavy masonry fireplace to retain the heat of the fire and a low ceiling to keep the room warm and comfortable.

The 18th-century log-built crofter's cottage from Hornborga (TOP RIGHT) has living rooms, cowshed, and barn all in one L-shaped building. The roof is of straw thatch topped with turf.

The old town quarters (BOTTOM RIGHT) mainly from Södermalm in Stockholm comprise houses and workshops from the 18th to 19th centuries such as the bakery in the foreground and the goldsmith's workshop and the rich merchant's summer residence beyond.

Buildings from the Upper Tisza region of northwestern Hungary were the first to be reconstructed in the Hungarian Open Air Museum at Szentendre, near Budapest. Cheap and abundant local materials characterized the early 19th-century oak-framed cottage, stable, and woodshed (LEFT) from Kispálad. Note the movable roof of the hay store!

The timber buildings of the wet and hilly western Transdanubia region have steeply pitched half-hipped (cut-back) roofs (ABOVE) which were originally designed to allow open access to the loft. These have since been closed in by a wooden gable end, often finely carved.

The interior of the huge threshing barn from Tiszabecs (RIGHT) has a fine roof of hewn oak rafters and trusses, and thick covering of straw thatch.

TOP LEFT: *A traditional roofed apiary from Pusztafala, Hungary. Mud-plastered and whitewashed, with coiled-rope beehives, it stands near the hay barn and pig sty.*

BOTTOM LEFT: *Although the crofts in villages had a kitchen, it was the practice to have a separate oven outside the house, too. This fine example from Kispálad, with its thatched roof and chimney, is for baking bread.*

ABOVE: *In 1880, a well-to-do Hungarian farmer and owner of 24 acres added two rooms to his house at Süttör, near Lake Fertö. One of these was the bedroom (SHOWN HERE), furnished with ornate four-poster beds. Low* tuli *(truckle beds) could be wheeled out from underneath these for the older children.*

LEFT: *Traditional village homes in South Korea were often built in an "L" or "U" shape around a courtyard. They were usually one-storey, timber-framed buildings with clay walls and thatched roofs. The 19th-century farmer's house from Yongkwangkun (reconstructed in the Korean Folk Village) has a raised verandah along one side where meals are taken during the summer. The wide overhanging thatched roof gives good protection to the walls and also provides storage space plus drying area for crops such as maize and peppers.*

ABOVE: *The Ullung Island in South Korea is subject to long winters, heavy snowfalls, rain, and wind. In this exposed spot the inhabitants developed a special design – "a house within a house". Protected by a thick outer structure of reeds or straw, the inner home was built of log walls and ceilings with clay chinking. Smoke from the kitchen was channelled under the earth floor and into the roof space where crops, such as potatoes, were stored, thus better preserving them and maintaining the home temperature.*

Bambooware (ABOVE) is a speciality of Tamyang in the southern Choila province of Korea. Hats, baskets, screens, fans, and boxes, dyed in many colours, have always been one of the country's sustainable village industries. Silk is another famous product. The whole process from silkworm raising to weaving is carried out by farming families as a sideline. Silk thread (LEFT) is released from cocoons set in boiling water and spun ready for weaving.

LEFT: Tanch'ong *is the intricate pattern-ing that has been painted on buildings since the Koguryo kingdom of 668–37* BC. *Usually in blue, yellow, red, white, and black, the designs were believed to ward off evil forces and bring good fortune. During the Koryo era, green and red became dominant.*

CENTRE: *The layout of the Toksu-gung Palace in Seoul built in the mid-15th century by King Sejo owes much to Chinese geomancy. Its walled compounds follow a N-S*

alignment, with the royal power issuing from the main south gate.

RIGHT: *Before entering a traditional Korean home, visitors placed their shoes on the* didimdol *or threshold step. From the raised wooden verandah, sliding screen doors, covered with mulberry paper, gave access to the compact rooms within. In these multi-function spaces (used for dining, working, relaxing, and sleeping), warmth came from the* ondol *floor.*

The Taos Pueblo (BELOW) in New Mexico is a cellular structure with many individual rooms built side by side and up to five storeys high. Originally, there were no doors or windows, and entry to each room was from the roof using removable ladders. The pueblo is constructed entirely of adobe – earth mixed with water and straw which is then poured into forms or made into sun-dried bricks. On top of the thick adobe walls, the floors and roofs are supported by large timbers or "vigas", hauled from the mountains, and smaller cross-timbers or "latillas" covered with brush and packed earth. Outside surfaces are regularly replastered with mud, while inside walls (LEFT) are whitewashed with gypsum. The corner fireplace is of Spanish influence; before its introduction, smoke escaped through the roof hatch. Today, ancient Indian rites and Catholicism are practised without conflict as evidenced by the presence of kivas and the Chapel of San Geronimo (RIGHT) in the same village.

LEFT: *Courtyards giving peace and privacy from the hubbub of city life have been an enduring building feature of many cultures. But they also have important environmental functions in providing coolness in summer and shelter in winter. By doing so, the courtyard helps to make the whole surrounding building more comfortable throughout the year. A superb example, at the heart of the 11th to 15th century churches of Santo Stefano in Bologna, Italy, is the Cortile di Pilato (SHOWN HERE), named after the curious marble basin called "Pilate's wash-hand bowl" in the courtyard centre.*

ABOVE: *When the French laid out the Vieux Carré (old quarter) in New Orleans in the 18th and 19th centuries, they followed Spanish-style town design. The buildings were built flush with the "banquette" (pavement), but to the rear they had attractive cool courtyards or patios filled with the lush vegetation of the region. Noted European architects Gallier (father and son), Latrobe (who helped to design the Capitol in Washington), the De Pouilly brothers, and the Dakins created memorable designs, making New Orleans in the 1840s one of the most imposing cities in North America.*

There are many traditional ways of shading buildings and rooms that are both simple and effective. Take, for example, the window shutters in Bologna, Italy (LEFT), with their vibrant colours, or the vine-covered balcony of a house in the white-painted "chora" of Ios, Greece (ABOVE). In both cases, as the streets in the old centres are narrow and winding, the summer sun can penetrate only briefly around noon. For the rest of the day, the buildings help shade each other. Inside, rooms are kept cool during the hottest part of the day by closing the shutters, windows, and curtains, and opening them only in the cool of the evening and at night.

Many of the older streets around the university campus in
Berkeley, California, have a pleasant vernacular feel
created by the timber-built houses shaded by mature trees
and thick creepers. (Many were built, however, of redwood
– now a scarce resource.) The fine early example (ABOVE),
with its generous bay windows and sitting-out porch, is
dramatically flanked by huge palms.

FIVE

CULTURAL IDENTITY

"We have to know from where we are coming to know where we are going."
CHARLES CORREA

It is the synthesis of past and present that has been the preoccupation of many architects in developing countries for the past three decades. On the one hand, Western industrial society has spawned international architectural images, modern technology, and new materials to build anonymous slab block apartments, airports, factories, and large hotels often ill-adapted to local social and climatic conditions. On the other hand, there are the strong regional cultural traditions of indigenous building using vernacular knowledge, forms, and materials that have proved well adapted to the locality for thousands of years. To Western-oriented eyes, the former is seen as inevitable "progress" toward a rich and educated urban modern world; the latter, as a regressive past associated with rural poverty, ignorance, and peasant culture. Until recently, internationalism has been the dominant trend, but with the rise of cultural pride in Asia, Africa, and Eastern Europe, and campaigns for recognition of ancient ethnic and territorial rights of Indian cultures in North and South America, local identity is re-emerging. But how can or should architects and designers, working against this background, try to resolve these polarities? Can there be a creative blend of Western technology and traditional forms? What is "authentic" architecture?

In the 1980s the Aga Khan Awards for Architecture, together with the influential quarterly *MIMAR – Architecture in Development*,* were launched to encourage discussion of these questions and to promote some of the best examples of modern architecture in the developing world. "It is my belief," says former MIMAR editor Hasan-Uddin Khan, "that architecture rooted in cultures and traditions must extend them to reflect contemporary concerns and expectations." He feels that rather than looking backward, we need to *transform* the models of the past to act as a catalyst for the future.

*Sadly, MIMAR magazine is no longer published.

"Tradition and modernity," he maintains, "are merely two sides of the same coin – and must be dealt with simultaneously. Building cannot be a rigid dogma, but a living, organic, ecological project. It is about continuity, based on memory, common sense, and experience, and is the foundation of invention."

In the New World there are moves afoot among indigenous peoples trained in Western architecture to reconnect modern design with their traditional cultures. In New Mexico, for example, a new Pueblo centre near Santa Fe is planned based on detailed surveys of the ancient Chaco Canyon pueblos, such as Pueblo Bonito. An innovative design office is to be set up within the centre staffed by local Indian designers who will be trained in modern applications of traditional cultural forms and techniques. Similar examples of this are to be found in Mexico, where Luis Barragan and Emilio Ambasz are combining Mexican indigenous knowledge and eco-design in a colourful and vigorous manner. A reawakening of cultural identity is one of the strongest and most hopeful themes in the rebirth of natural architecture.

Proposed Poeh Center at the Pojoaque Pueblo, New Mexico.

Hassan Fathy It was in the wake of "Westernization" of the Middle East and the spread of an alien architecture, totally inappropriate to both climate and culture, that Egyptian architect Hassan Fathy found his mission. As an early protagonist of the value of diverse Arab and Islamic cultures, he realized the urgent need to preserve and develop these for the modern Arab world. He was inspired by the ancient Egyptian buildings, their continuity of tradition, and the practical yet sophisticated knowledge of the *muallims*, the anonymous master builders. Using local materials to hand, particularly mud-brick, and traditional building forms such as internal courtyards and vaulted and domed roofs, they had produced, over thousands of years, an indigenous architecture that Fathy knew was just as relevant today. What especially surprised and pleased him were the comfort and tranquillity these apparently simple structures provided in the harsh climatic conditions of the Middle East. This was not via modern hi-tech air-conditioning but by understanding and using the natural physical properties of heat, wind, and water – the "natural environmental controls." Fathy himself was to employ these natural properties very successfully in his own designs, which he later described in his book *Natural Energy and Vernacular Architecture*.

He first incorporated these elements in simple prototype courtyard houses and then designed many ingenious projects for both rich and poor. But it was his experiences with the poor that intrigued and taught him the most. In his classic book *Architecture for the Poor*, he relates how he saw that an answer to housing for the future lay in the roots of the past:

"The peasant built his house out of mud, or mud-bricks, which he dug out of the ground and dried in the sun. And here, in every hovel in Egypt, was the answer to my problem. Here, for years, for centuries, the peasant had been wisely and quietly exploiting the obvious building materials, while we, with our modern school-learned ideas, never dreamed of using such a ludicrous substance as mud for so serious a creation as a house."

Hassan Fathy's work has had a strong influence far beyond Egypt and he has many followers working today to develop his ideas and projects even further.

Francisco "Bobby" Mañosa "A vision of a future Filipino architecture in our country cannot help but open doors to an awareness, assimilation and acceptance of indigenous materials, and our vernacular heritage generally."

The Mañosa residence, Metro Manila, in the Philippines is inspired by the traditional nipa *hut.*

For Filipino architect Bobby Mañosa, the new awakening of Filipino culture after four centuries of colonial rule has naturally led to a search for a new national identity in architecture. It is vital in countries such as the Philippines to research and identify one's own cultural heritage to find out what can be applied today. It is important not only to know how indigenous materials such as bamboo, coconut, rattan, *cogon*, and *nipa* were used in the past and how they are used today, but also how they can be improved and developed, via new technologies, to meet present-day needs. By doing so, Mañosa feels that prejudices against older materials can be overcome and exciting new possibilities created.

Bamboo, for instance, is a plentiful and obvious material but considered by most people to be of "poor" quality, technically and socially. But using modern research to improve durability, and incorporating it in sound, innovative, and aesthetically appealing designs, Mañosa has done much to transform popular opinion of the material. In this way he has helped to re-introduce it as an economical and sustainable resource, ideal for structure, finishes, and furniture.

The traditional elevated humble *nipa* huts, or *bahay kubo*, were built instinctively to suit the local climate and terrain. Their steep wide-eaved roofs, *tukod* windows, and walls built of woven dried grass kept the interiors water-tight and well ventilated. Mañosa sees these and other vernacular forms as repositories of profound meaning and beauty and as starting points for what he describes as "the propagation of tradition and craftsmanship, which far from being irrelevant relics of the past, express the true soul of the Filipino, synthesising the genius of the Malay civilization of which we are part."

Charles Correa "By the year 2000, there will be almost 50 cities in the world each with over 15 million inhabitants: 40 will be in the Third World, most of these in Asia, and one of them will be Bombay."

Working mostly as a public architect in India but now of world renown, Charles Correa sees a future dominated by increasing human population. Because of this he feels that events are more likely to be determined in the East than in the West. Working in this urgent context he has devoted much of his career to trying to find solutions (or, at least, remedies) to the enormous problems of urban and shanty-town growth. His plans for New Bombay attempt to divert migrant newcomers to the hinterland, linking new low-cost housing by public transport to the old centre. However, although deeply committed to these problems, he draws much of his inspiration from traditional values, such as those embodied in the small Indian village, so central to Gandhi's philosophy. Here he seems to find a natural empathy and grounding for his work in the ecological systems and the ancient rural pattern of village life. This and the Indian climate, with its heat and monsoons, have guided many of his housing designs such as the "tube house" type from which many variations have been developed, from low-cost, low-rise cluster housing to the impressive Kovalam Hotel, Kerala.

The way earlier civilizations in India built for the climate has many important messages for Correa and modern architecture. The Red Forts of the Mogul Empire at Agra and Delhi show what he calls a tendency to *disaggregate* architectural forms. Thus there are the separate pavilions at the top of the forts set in terraced gardens with fountains and canals, and below are the sunken courts and rooms.

> "*In the early morning of the summer months* [writes Correa] *a velvet shamiana* [canopy] *was stretched over the rim of the courtyards trapping the cold overnight air in the level of the rooms. This was where the Mughal emperor spent his day. In the evening the shamiana was removed, and the emperor and his court came out on the gardens and pavilions of the terrace level. In the cold but sunny winters, the pattern was reversed.*"

Via his design philosophy of "transfer and transformation", Correa re-integrates many older fundamental ideas, such as this one, into his modern designs, which recognize the problems of today yet show a deep respect for India's culture and traditions.

One of Hassan Fathy's best-known projects is the village of
New Gourna in Upper Egypt. Built in 1948, it was
planned to rehouse the 7000 inhabitants of Old Gourna,
many of whom were known robbers of the ancient tombs
at nearby Luxor. It was a bold early attempt to transpose
European concepts of "new towns" into the Arab world
and promote generic building forms, local materials, and
construction methods. But the experiment was overtaken
by the massive migration of the rural poor to Cairo and
was never the success it could have been; in the end, it
provided housing to squatters displaced by the Aswan
Dam. However, the mosque (ABOVE), which is the focal
point of the village, remains today the best-loved and
maintained public building. Based on solid massive forms
of Nubian traditional design, Fathy used mud brick for
walls, roof vaults, and the dome.

Hassan Fathy adapted the courtyard house forms of Cairo as the typical housing unit for New Gourna. Although justifiable on environmental and health grounds, the transfer to rural Upper Egypt did not immediately suit local social norms where courtyard houses were usually the preserve of wealthier families. Nevertheless, these experimental houses confirmed Fathy's belief that local vernacular forms and spatial arrangements had many lessons for modern Egyptian architecture and environmental design. In his words:

"If possible, I want to bridge the gulf that separates folk architecture from architect's architecture. I always wanted to provide some solid and visible link between these two architectures in the shape of features, common to both, in which the people could find a familiar point of reference from which to enlarge their understanding of the new, and which the architect could use to test the truth of his work in relation to people and place."

The felling of the tropical forests in the Philippines has been so severe that there is little left of them today. Responding to this, Filipino architect Bobby Mañosa has focused his attention on bamboo as an alternative. "Bamboo is the only plant," says Mañosa, "that can grow fast enough to cope with the growing demand for present and future housing. But unless we apply new found technology and encourage willingness and acceptance by the people, it cannot prove its worth." As a personal answer to the tragedies following the eruption of the Pinatubo Volcano, Mañosa developed low-cost bamboo housing. Working closely with a company called Intechdev, a new product, "plyboo" (bamboo plywood), was developed as a major building component.

When asked to design accommodation for the Pearl Farm Resort in the southern Philippines (ABOVE and RIGHT), Mañosa saw another opportunity to use bamboo. With the full support of his clients, he based his bamboo design on the traditional Samal house, which is built on stilts over the water. "Surprisingly bamboo lends a very contemporary look," comments Mañosa, "and serves to unify the development. No other structure in the entire country today can speak so extensively about the application of this material."

The Belapur Housing, New Bombay, India, completed in 1986, combines many of the themes of Charles Correa's architecture: equity, incrementality, and pluralism. "Open-to-sky" and "disaggregated" spaces encourage the inhabitants to create their own environments combined with income-generating activities. Built for a hundred lower- and middle-income families, each unit has its own plot to enable the family to extend or change the house to meet their needs and wishes; their simple construction facilitating ease of alteration by local masons and the families themselves. The low-rise high-density plan uses a cluster arrangement around small community spaces (RIGHT). These clusters combine with each other to make neigbourhoods served by schools and other public facilities.

The traditional buildings of India were inventively designed to take advantage of prevailing breezes and light. The Royal Pavilion at the old Padmanabhapuram Palace in the hot humid climate of southern India was built as a stepped pyramid covered with a tile pitched roof. This design not only kept out the sun and rain but deflected the line of sight downward to the cool surrounding grass. Correa used the same principle at the Bay Island Hotel in the Andaman Islands (built 1979–82) where a series of pavilions with wide overhanging roofs step down toward the sea. Ranged around courtyards, the pavilions are connected by covered walkways (ABOVE).

The vernacular of the Canary Islands
is a mixture of many styles: Moorish
"Mudéjar", Gothic, Renaissance, and
Spanish. One typical feature is the
lattice-screen wooden balcony such as
the beautiful one (LEFT) at the
Instituto Cabrera Pinto, La Laguna,
Tenerife. In recent times, the Canaries
have suffered from innumerable
developments of large hotels and

tourist resorts. *Crusading against this trend, architect, painter, and sculptor César Manrique has spent much of his life trying to preserve the landscape and use traditional features in modern design, such as the simple wooden fencing* (ABOVE). *Certainly his humour was far from lacking when he set these uprooted palms* (RIGHT) *on end!*

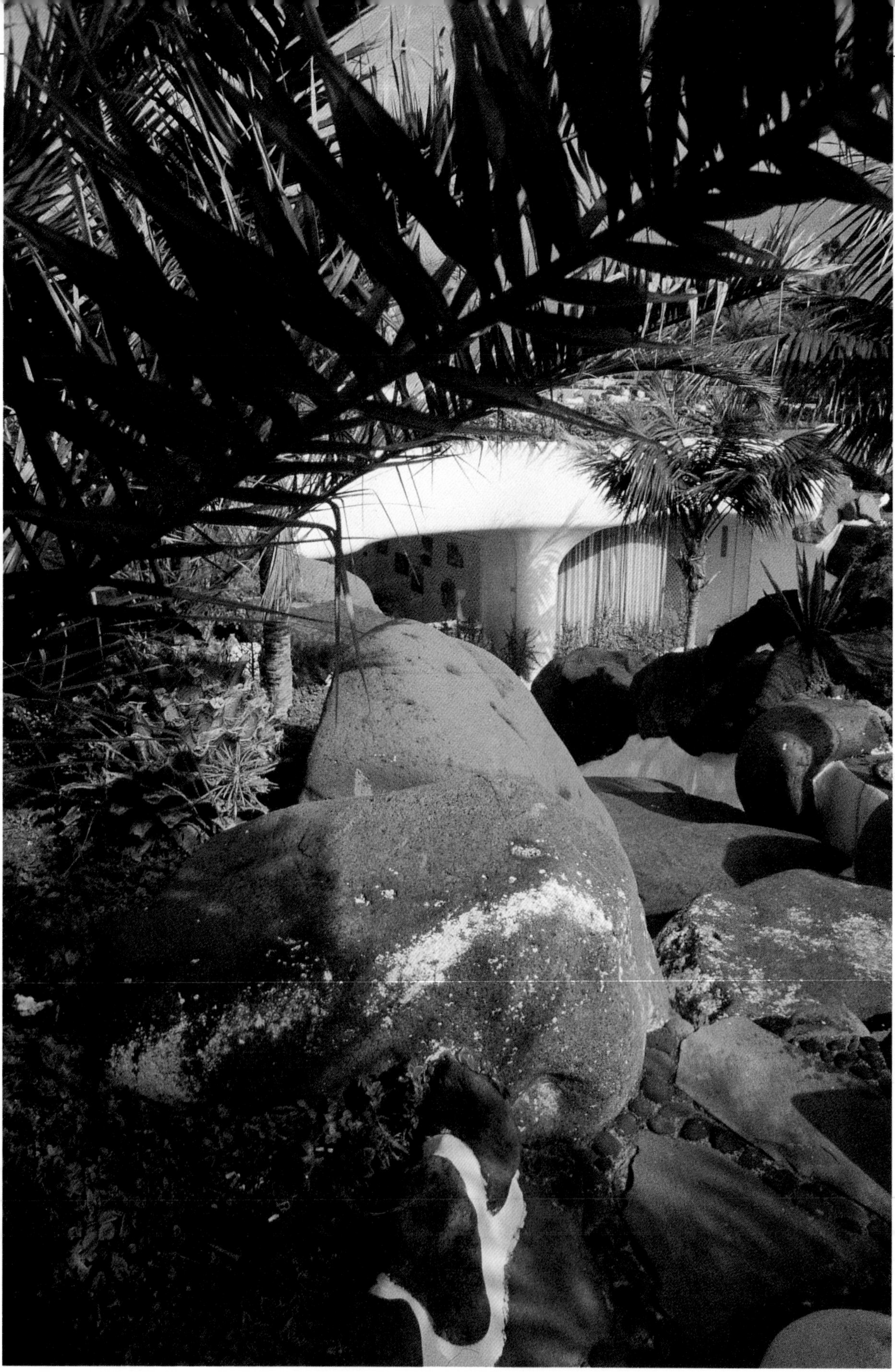

One of Manrique's most famous and
successful projects in Tenerife is the
Costa de Martiánez and Lido in
Puerto de la Cruz, completed in 1977.
Here he designed the whole seafront
promenade using native details such
as the simple wooden pale fencing
(SEE PP132–3).

In the Lido San Telmo, a large sea-
water lake with islands of lava rock
and small swimming pools is set
among palms, creeper-shaded loggias
(ABOVE), and green lawns. Underground buildings (FAR LEFT) echo
older cave dwellings (NEAR LEFT).

In June 1990, a Lutheran church (known to the local congregation as "Christ's boat") was inaugurated in the Hungarian holiday resort of Siófok on Lake Balaton. Using images from nature, Christianity, and Transylvanian mythology, the design of Imre Makovecz makes it one of the most significant and striking buildings in the area (BELOW and RIGHT). The interior timber (FAR LEFT) was donated by the cathedral church of Oulu, Finland. The "Tree of Life" cross (LEFT) symbolizes life overcoming death.

The Roman Catholic church at Paks, Hungary, completed in 1987, is perhaps one of the most successful of Imre Makovecz's designs yet. It combines in a passionate and masterful way the underlying themes of his life's work. In its powerful forms Makovecz expresses Hungary's newfound freedom from oppression and its cultural and spiritual renewal, now that individuals have the right to self-expression and worship. The architecture's ethnic language and use of natural materials convey a continuity with the past and a harmony with the environment.

The flowing forms and spaces of Makovecz's organic architecture boldly link earth to spirit. The striking triple-spired bell tower (LEFT) aspires to Moon, Sun, and God. The sculptural tree forms (ABOVE) branch beside the nave rising from columns fashioned from whole trees. For Makovecz, they symbolize our reach toward heaven, while our roots remain firmly planted in the ground. Even the rounded form of the nave, which is partly earth-covered (BOTTOM RIGHT), contrasts with the heavenward thrust of the angel, lightly poised in front with outstretched wings (ABOVE RIGHT).

The Mogyoróhegy recreation area at Visegrád, Hungary, includes a campsite, restaurant, centre for nature education, playing fields, and a forester's residence.

In the centre for nature education, Imre Makovecz expresses the relation of humanity with nature. The turf-covered dome (BELOW LEFT) resembles a huge natural mound and is topped by a crown, pierced by arched windows. It has an entrance flanked by great wing-like doors (ABOVE LEFT). Inside, the sun shines through a central skylight and plays across a sun dial. Makovecz has a great love and respect for Hungary's native buildings. He has made many studies of its traditional forms and constructions, and is always struck by their simplicity, and the commonsense and inventiveness of their makers.

The forester's house, with cafeteria annex, is part vernacular and part modern. The house is based on a traditional farmhouse with its courtyard and pleasant whitewashed arcades (BELOW). However, the cafeteria annex (RIGHT) is unashamedly modern. Its storey-high glazed wall literally cuts through old traditions as it slices through the facade, with a surprising and tongue-in-cheek splash of modernity!

Earth has been a basic building material for thousands of years. In North America, traditional earth buildings include native American pit houses, earth lodges, and pueblos; plains settlers' sod houses; and Spanish adobe homes. Earth is now being rediscovered as an attractive modern building material with many environmental advantages, being abundant, durable, energy-efficient, and often recyclable. Leading exponents, designer/ builder David Easton and landscape/interior designer Cynthia Wright of Rammed Earth Works, California, have improved traditional techniques to exceed California's strict earthquake and energy conservation standards. The Energywise Showcase Home in Napa (ABOVE and RIGHT), sponsored by the Pacific General & Electric Company, has 24-inch (60-centimetre) earth walls (stabilized with 10% cement), needs no air conditioning, and requires only minimal winter heating (SEE ALSO OVERLEAF).

CONTINUED FROM PREVIOUS PAGE: *Inside, the home feels solid and comfortable, the earth walls imaginatively stratified with warm reds and browns. Earth is also used for floor tiles and countertops. New, environment-friendlier cotton roof insulation and double-paned low-emissivity glass windows conserve energy. Outside, shade is provided by verandahs, trees, and vines.*

SIX

LIVING THE DREAM

It is not enough to talk, write, or dream about change. Once the idea is there, it is natural to want to go further – in fact, to live the dream. All over the world there are intriguing examples of people who have taken that step toward an ecological lifestyle and started a process that has not only affected themselves but has changed others and the world beyond. This chapter concerns individuals and their projects rather than architects and their buildings.

For every example given in this book, there are scores of others in every country where individuals, families, organizations, and even whole communities are making the transformation to living once more in harmony with the earth. Very often people feel daunted by the world around them and think that they are powerless to affect its course. Global environmental efforts, such as those co-ordinated by the United Nations Earth Summit, even though they do involve grass roots participants, still seem remote, perhaps to most people. This is why the smaller individual efforts are so important, and, in Ernst Schumacher's famous phrase, "beautiful". They demonstrate just how much can be achieved and how small beginnings can lead to large and widespread effects. The examples that follow show how different individuals and small groups in different places have been successful in finding a way and how they are influencing others around them. They haven't always found it easy – trying out new ideas rarely is – but they have found it satisfying. These examples give an impression of some of the excitement that can come with change and offer inspiration to others to follow suit. They demonstrate that it is worth taking the first step ourselves, or joining with others, to put our ideas into action; to make our dreams a reality and establish our link from earth to spirit.

Bamberton, Canada

Billed to become North America s most habitable and ecologically responsible new town, Bamberton will be located on the Saanich Inlet near Victoria, British Columbia. The 1560-acre (630-hectare) site is planned in 20 years to house 12,000 people. The developer, South Island Development Cooperative, is owned by four large trade union pension funds.

Community recycling, environmentally sound building materials, energy-efficient designs and transport are all essential ingredients. "In Bamberton" sums up Guy Dauncey, project environmental consultant, "we are doing whatever we can, within the limits of our knowledge, to ensure that Bamberton makes an ecologically sustainable contribution to the region and sets an example for Canada, for North America, and for the Earth as a whole. It is an idea whose time has come."

Crystal Waters, Australia

Australia's first intentional permaculture village is situated north of Brisbane, Queensland, near the Conondale Range National Park. This beautiful 640-acre (260-hectare) site has high rainfall and warm winters, making it ideal for growing fruit and vegetables. Under the plan drawn up by Max Lindegger and Robert Tap (later joined by others), 300 people are to settle in more than 80 housing lots. (By mid-1993, approximately 160 were resident.)

Steep ridges and gullies are being reforested, the slopes below are being used for mixed grazing, orchards, and forestry, while the fertile river and creek flats serve for intensive horticulture. With "Care for the Earth, Care for People and Dispersal of Surpluses" as the code to live by, elected "elders" to resolve disputes, business co-ops, and a "People's Bank" at nearby Maleny, Crystal Waters is an exciting model for future sustainable settlements.

Windowcraft, Sweden

When Hans Allback worked as a decorator in Sweden, he began to suffer from allergies and poor health. He slowly realized that it was the harmful substances contained within the synthetic chemical paints he was using that were the root of the trouble. Out of work with no money, he and his wife Sonja decided to start a new business renovating old timber windows. Twelve years on, Hans and Sonja have built a unique and successful business which now also involves their two daughters. Traditional crafts and materials are combined with modern methods to achieve economical and environmentally sound window restoration, re-using as much original material as possible. With this combined approach, the Allbacks created a new profession, which they called "windowcraft".

A windowcraftsperson is a carpenter, glazier, painter, blacksmith, and bricklayer, all in one, and understands the interaction between all the materials involved. Every window is regarded as a single unit, to be treated in a single workshop by a single craftsperson. Using their patented infrared putty lamp, the Allbacks can soften rock-hard old putty to allow any original hand-blown glass to be re-used. In their workshops they have developed many special tools and methods to make timber window restoration competitive with plastic and aluminium windows. Their own linseed oil putty and paints, made to original formulae, have proved to be longer-lasting and far more economical than modern synthetic paint equivalents. By enrolling on their diploma training courses, many people have become qualified in this new craft. Starting from small beginnings, the Allbacks' new business venture is spreading fast.

Urban Ecology, USA

For Richard Register, starting Urban Ecology "was an exciting adventure for most of us, many of the early activists having roots in Paolo Soleri's experiment in the high desert of Arizona, the car-less, aspiring ecological town called Arcosanti."

It was in 1975, on his return from Arcosanti, that the talented ecotheorist Richard Register cofounded Urban Ecology in an attempt to steer Berkeley, California, toward ecologically healthy development. "The whole time we added up one accomplishment after another, a creek restoration here, a tree planting there, a solar greenhouse in one part of the town, a 'slow street' promoting bicycles and discouraging cars somewhere else . . . All the while we thought we were adding pieces of the picture that would coalesce in the minds of our fellow citizens into a vision of the ecological city."

To help this process Richard wrote his influential book *Ecocity Berkeley: Building Cities for a Healthy Future*. In 1990 Urban Ecology organized the First International Ecocity Conference in Berkeley and around 800 people attended. Inspired by this, Ecocity 2 took place in Adelaide, Australia, in 1992. Also in that year (and independently of Urban Ecology), ECO-URBS '92 was held in Brazil just before the UN Conference on Environment and Development. "But for all its successful projects and growing general knowledge of ecocity efforts," says Register, "the pieces of ecocity never coalesced in the mind of the public. Nowhere do enough ecocity features come together at a single glance. The conception of an ecologically healthy city is barely dawning among citizens of towns like Berkeley."

Urban Ecology, Richard Register, and his new organization, Ecocity Builders, are dedicated to the simultaneous construction of demonstration building development and nature restoration. Their work continues to make ecocities a reality.

A proposed "integral neighbourhood" in Berkeley would be like a village within a city.

CRATerre, France

The revival of earthen architecture (architecture based on adobe or sun-dried earth bricks) in France was started in 1973 by a group of students at the School of Architecture, Grenoble. Inspired by the rich tradition of earth building in the Rhône-Alpes region, they organized a special course and created an "Earth Laboratory". In 1979, they went on to found a non-profit-making organization known as Centre de Recherche et d'Application Terre – CRATerre. Following on from an influential international exhibition entitled "Down to Earth; Mud Architecture: an old idea, a new future", CRATerre demonstrated the modern uses of earth in a pilot project called "Domaine de la Terre". In this, 65 medium-rent houses were built in the new city of L'Isle d'Abeau, between Lyon and Chamery, using *pisé* or rammed earth walls. From these promising results, the French government has backed many more projects, now amounting to several thousands of completed earth-built houses.

"To improve housing conditions for underprivileged people" is one of CRATerre's aims, and with work, mainly in Africa and South America, they have trained local people to revive their own cultures of earth building. Today, via "Project Gaia", there is an international "Gaia Network" of professionals and experts in 29 countries, a "Gaia Research Index" of more than 2000 projects, and a 900-title bibliography, plus training courses and many live projects. These all go to make CRATerre one of the leading organizations in the world promoting the revival of earthen architecture.

Ecological Design Association (EDA), England

The EDA was founded by the author himself. In his own words: "It was obvious to me when I had just finished writing *The Natural House Book* that there were a lot of people out there doing fascinating things in ecology and healthy buildings that simply did not know of each other's existence or work in Britain and around the world. The book had taken two years of research and almost a year to write. I had been inspired by all the people who had helped and their endeavours. Together, they represented the fundamental seachange that was taking place in the world of design and building. A change little recognized, at the time, especially in Britain. One of these people was Stefan Bartha, Honorary Professor, Academy of Debrecen, a Hungarian engineer living in Sweden. In 1982, he cofounded the Association for Ecological Design with Bertram Broberg, a Swedish professor of solid

The author's house in inner London uses natural materials and plants to create a healthy indoor environment.

mechanics. An annual symposium had been held every year in Sweden and, more recently, in Hungary under the current President, Dutch architect Dr Peter Schmid. These were attended by participants from many design and other fields from all over the world; the warm friendly atmosphere attracting them back time and time again. In 1989, when I was invited to go, it became obvious to me that we needed something of the kind in Britain which would link people together at home and put them in touch with others abroad. An informal group of us soon met in London and the 'Ecological Design Association' – the EDA – was founded."

Monthly meetings covered association business and guest speakers or members were invited to talk. The meetings became larger and enthusiasm grew. In 1990, the EDA was publicly launched with an exhibition of members' work at the London Ecology Centre. The EDA is now a registered non-profit-making organization with more than 500 members. Links have been made with equivalent international design bodies, and various local branches in England, plus the Scottish Ecological Design Association (SEDA), have been formed to promote ecological design at the grass roots. In addition to its annual members' gathering, the EDA has hosted talks, seminars, workshops, and exhibitions, including lectures by internationally recognized designers and ecologists such as Victor Papanek. Through newsletters and its journal *EcoDesign*, Members' Directory, and information sheets, the EDA is a growing force in ecological design.

GAIA International

"GAIA International stands for the balance and integration of the built environment with ecosystems towards a sustainable way of life for all species of this planet."

In 1990 the Gaia Group in Norway invited participants from 12 countries to join them in forming an informal international network of like-minded architects, permaculturalists, and biologists. The gathering place was the quiet and beautiful village of Jøllestø on the southern coast of Norway; the adopted home and centre of the Gaia Group and their families. The three-day event covered presentations of the work, status, and problems of ecology and design in each country, and ended with a decision on future collaboration, a Statement of Intent (above), and dates for future annual meetings. Since then, the group's meetings, with some new members, have been hosted by members in Scotland, Sweden, and Denmark. Members of the group have collaborated in architectural competitions, courses, and workshops, and in 1992 the group was invited to speak at the Union of International Architects Conference on "Ecological Architecture" held in Stockholm and Helsinki.

Gaia Group, Norway

Gaia was formed in 1983 by a group of architects interested in an ecological approach to building and planning. Over the last ten years the group has grown to include other disciplines. They have an office in Oslo but their main centre is at a small settlement on the coast of southern Norway. Here, a few years ago, families in the group began to buy up old disused farmhouses and land, and laid the foundations for a remarkable working community. Experimental ideas, based on ecology and healthy building, were built into both their own homes and new prototypes for clients. Following permaculture principles, the group's aim was (and still is) to create holistic buildings that integrate with the natural environment, making them self-regulating ecological systems (SEE ECO-CYCLE HOUSE, P.91).

Healthy indoor climate is an important theme and various energy-efficient "breathing" constructions and ventilation methods have been

pioneered by the group. Combining craft and design skills, architects/carpenters Rolf Jacobsen and Dag Roalkvam not only design houses, they also build them. Others within the group include Bjørn Berge who writes books (so far, on sick housing and on ecological building materials), and incorporates his ideas into his house designs; Frederica Miller, who works from Oslo and concentrates more on the urban context and permaculture, recently helping the group to participate in the competition "Bergen – a Healthy City – 1995"; and Marianne Leisner, agronomist, and Wenche Ellingsen, biologist, who oversee permaculture planting and biological waste-water recycling. Architects Kjell Grimsaeth and Marianne Lund are also in the Gaia Group. In 1990, the Gaia Group initiated *Gaia International* to form a broader group with ecological designers drawn from 13 countries.

Each year, the Gaia group is hosted by different members in their own country. When it was Denmark's turn, the group met at Ross and Hildur Jackson's centre at Gaia Fjordvang in north Jutland (ABOVE). With design assistance from Floyd Stein and Hamish Stewart, the centre (home of the Gaia Trust) is planned to become a permaculture-based co-housing and working community. The original buildings have already been converted to offices and accommodation (LEFT) for visitors and course attendees.

Members, families, and guests of the Gaia International group (TOP RIGHT), assembled at its inaugural meeting at Gaia Lista (GL), Norway. Top row (left to right): Floyd Stein (Denmark), Bjørn Berge (GL), Max Lindegger (Australia), Kjell Grimsaeth (GL), Peter Schmid (Holland), David Pearson (England),

Dag Roalkvam (GL), Declan Kennedy (Germany). Middle row: Howard Liddell (Gaia Scotland), Marianne Lund (GL), Trudi Lindegger (Australia), Elaine Rigby (England), Frederica Miller (Gaia Oslo), Varis Bokalders (Sweden), Bertil Jonsson (Sweden), John Brennan (Gaia Scotland), Robert Laporte (USA). Bottom row: Ingurn Bruskeland and Chris Butters (Bhutan), Karen Zahle (Denmark), Wenche Ellingsen (GL), Margrit Kennedy (Germany), Rolf Jacobsen (GL), and Marianne Leisner (GL). Other members (not photographed) include Linton Ross (England), Paul Leech (Ireland), Bruno Erat (Finland), and Joachim Eble (Germany).

Centre for Alternative Technology, Wales (CAT)

Not satisfied with simply talking about environmental problems, a group of campaigners in the 1970s decided to set up a centre to research and demonstrate sustainable living. They found a disused slate quarry and with almost no money but volunteer help created a unique 40-acre (16-hectare) "green" educational and visitor centre. Now of international renown, CAT attracts over 70,000 visitors a year.

Many of the 30 permanent staff – engineers, architects, builders, teachers, horticulturalists, biologists, environmentalists, and others – live and work on site with their families. Although not totally self-sufficient, they concern themselves as much with energy production as with energy saving and try to show that comfortable lifestyles are possible using far less energy and fewer resources. In fact, the centre is not connected to mains electricity and produces its needs via sun, wind, and water power.

A water-powered cliff railway or a woodland walk takes you up the steep slope to the main displays. These include low-energy and self-build houses, a wide range of wind-, solar-, and water-power systems, extensive organic gardens with farm animals and fish pond, plus a wholefood restaurant, book and gift shop and children's recycling centre and adventure playground.

They learn much from experiments; a solar or trombe wall for the staff cottages' space heating, for instance (FAR LEFT), has not proved as effective as hoped due to the cloudy Welsh weather and its tree-lined valley location. But the "eco-cabins" (NEAR LEFT) are a very successful educational development allowing schoolchildren hands-on experience of running an eco-house. They have to cut their own wood, cook for themselves, make compost, cultivate their own garden plots, use a biological sewage treatment plant (BELOW LEFT), and even turf-roof their own cabins!

Urban Ore, California

There is a growing number of "reclamation centres" for second-hand building materials and equipment, such as this one in Berkeley, California, where anything from wash basins (ABOVE) to doors and windows (LEFT) can be purchased for a fraction of the price of the new article. Very often, older goods are better made and more robust than newer ones, and by re-using them you not only save resources but have fun in owning something with some character and history.

When Annelies Schönek and Elsemari (Maja) Malmgren started a small community at Almågarden Farm, Lunger, Arborga, Sweden, they did not realize that it would take over a hundred volunteers working in five sessions to complete the large community house they now occupy. Its exterior appearance and interior layout closely follow the traditional farmhouses of the area. But its solid timber frame has 18-inch (45-centimetre)-thick insulating walls built of "leichtlehm" – a light-weight mixture of rye straw, clay-earth, sand, horse manure, and water – rammed between shutters which are then removed. Outside, it is clad in timber and inside, finished with lime or clay plaster. They are continuing to construct buildings using "leichtlehm" such as the biological toilet (ABOVE LEFT and RIGHT), and are experimenting with other methods. Their organic gardens provide wholesome food and their looms produce beautiful cloth from hand-dyed wools.

Paul Bierman-Lytle, an architect who has pioneered healthy building in the US, has also founded, with Paul Novack, the Environmental Construction Outfitters. Their SoHo showroom, Manhattan (ABOVE), provides easier access to the supply of healthy and environmentally sound building materials, services, and technologies.

"Our philosophy is about living more simply," says Katherine Tiddens, owner of Terra Verde, an "ecological department store" also in SoHo (ABOVE). Both the impressive range of merchandise and the construction of the store (influenced by Bill McDonough) are as environmentally correct and healthy as possible.

The many earth-sheltered solar buildings of architect Malcolm Wells, such as his own home at Brewster, Massachusetts (RIGHT), are ample witness of his desire to live his dream of a "gentle architecture": "a gentler, smaller-scaled, decentralized architecture with its emphasis on natural systems – natural ventilation, natural lighting, natural treatment of wastes, natural heating and air conditioning . . ."

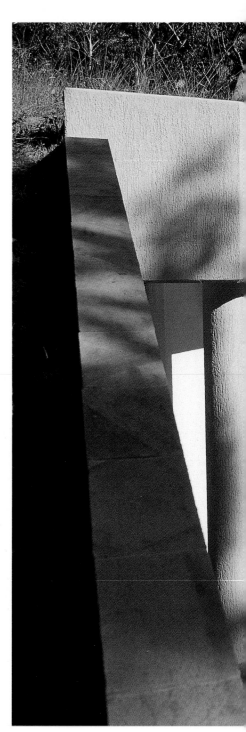

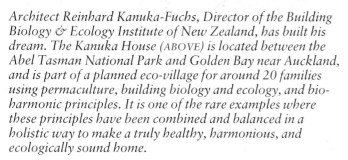

Architect Reinhard Kanuka-Fuchs, Director of the Building Biology & Ecology Institute of New Zealand, has built his dream. The Kanuka House (ABOVE) is located between the Abel Tasman National Park and Golden Bay near Auckland, and is part of a planned eco-village for around 20 families using permaculture, building biology and ecology, and bio-harmonic principles. It is one of the rare examples where these principles have been combined and balanced in a holistic way to make a truly healthy, harmonious, and ecologically sound home.

The columns of the facade are scaled to echo the tall straight trees that surround Ecaspace 3 (ABOVE), a large bushland residence on the central coast of New South Wales. Designed by Australian architect Dr Sydney Baggs, a well-known proponent of earth-sheltered building, it is built into the hillside with its entrance courtyard on the sun-facing side. Sun-controlled glass walls, plus the ambient earth temperatures, maintain a comfortable indoor environment throughout the year, while non-toxic natural finishes make this a low-allergy house, too.

Resources

AGA KHAN AWARDS FOR ARCHITECTURE

The Aga Khan Trust for Culture
32 Crêts-de-Pregny, CH-1218, Grand-Saconnex,
Geneva, Switzerland

Aga Khan Foundation (USA)
1901 L St NW, Suite 700, Washington DC 20036

ORGANIZATIONS

Association for Ecological Design
PO Box 27, S-233 00, Svedala, Sweden

Building Biology & Ecology Institute of New
Zealand
PO Box 2764, 22 Customs St West, Auckland,
New Zealand

Centre for Alternative Technology
Machynlleth, Powys SY20 9AZ, Wales

CRATerre-EAG
BP 53 F-38090, Villefontaine, France

Crystal Waters Permaculture Village
MS 16, Maleny 4552, Australia

Ecological Design Association
The British School
Slad Rd, Stroud, Glos. GL5 1QW, England

Fundacion César Manrique
Taro De Tahiche, 35509 Tesquise Teno,
Lanzarote, Canary Islands

Gaia Fjordvang
Skyumvej 101, Snedsted, 7752 Denmark

International Institute for Bau-Biologie &
Ecology Inc.
PO Box 387, Clearwater, Florida, FL 34615

Scottish Ecological Design Association
c/o Royal Institute of Architects in Scotland,
15 Rutland Sq, Edinburgh EH1 2BE, Scotland

Urban Ecology Inc.
PO Box 10144, Berkeley, California, CA 94709

COMPANIES

Environmental Construction Outfitters
44 Crosby St, New York, NY 10021

Fönster Hantverkarna AB
Bjäresjö Skola, S-271 91 Ystad, Sweden
(windowcraft renovation)

South Island Development Cooperative
Suite 550, 2950 Douglas St, Victoria, British
Columbia, Canada V8T 4N4
(Bamberton)

Terra Verde Trading Company
120 Wooster St, New York City, 10012

Turkoman Gers, Arlington Mill, Bibury, Glos.
GL7 5NL, England
(yurts)

Urban Ore
7th St & Gilman Avenue, Berkeley, California

ARCHITECTS AND CONSULTANTS

Ton Alberts
Architechenbureau Alberts & van Huut,
Keizergracht, 169 1016 Amsterdam, The
Netherlands

Paul Bierman-Lytle
The Masters Corporation, PO Box 514, 289 Mill
Road, New Canaan, CT 06840

Charles Correa
9 Mathew Rd, Bombay 400 004, India

Croxton Collaborative
1122 Madison Avenue, New York, NY 10028

Debra Dadd-Redalia
PO Box 279, Forest Knolls, CA 94933

Joachim Eble
Berliner Ring 47a, DW-7400, Tübingen, Germany

ECA Space Design Pty. Ltd.
4 de Villiers Avenue, Chatswood,
2067, Australia

Gaia-Lista
Jøllestø, 4560 Vanse, Norway

Gaia-Oslo
Skovveien 49, N-0258 Oslo, Norway

Phil Hawes & Associates
PO Box 1389, Oracle, AR 85623
(Biosphere 2)

James T Hubbell
930 Orchard Lane, Santa Ysabel, CA 92070

Paul Leech
Gaia Associates, 11 Upper Mount St, Dublin 2,
Eire

Howard Liddell
Gaia Architects, Aberfeldy Studios, Chapel St,
Aberfeldy, Perthshire PH15 2AW, Scotland

Francisco Mañosa & Ptnrs
PO Box 92 Greenhills, Metro Manila, Philippines

William McDonough Associates
116 E 27th Street, New York, NY 10016

Victor Papanek
The University of Kansas, School of Architecture
and Urban Design, 417 Marvin Hall, Lawrence,
Kansas 66045-2250

Bart Prince
3501 Monte Vista NE, Albuquerque, New Mexico
87106

Prisma Arkitekter
PO Box 119, 153 22 Järna, Sweden

Rammed Earth Works
1058 Second Avenue, Napa, CA 94558

Peter Schmid
Technical University Eindhoven, PO Box 513,
5600 MB Eindhoven, The Netherlands

Solar Survival Architecture
PO Box 1041, Taos, New Mexico 87571
(Earthships)

Paolo Soleri
Arcosanti, 6433 Doubletree Rd, Scottsdale, AZ
85253

Carol Venolia
PO Box 369, Gualala, CA 95445

Malcolm Wells
PO Box 1149, Brewster, MA 02631

John Wilkes
Virbela Flow Design Research Group, Emerson
College, Forest Row, Sussex RH18 5JX, England
(flow forms)

Jonathan Yardley
PO Box 960, Ganges, British Columbia, VO5
1EO, Canada

Bibliography

Bjørn Berge, *De Siste Syke Hus*,
Universitetsforlaget, Norway, 1988

Bjørn Berge, *Bygnings Materialenes Okologi*,
Universitetsforlaget, Norway, 1992

John Bower, *The Healthy House*, Stuart Lyle, New
York, 1989

Julian Burger, *The Gaia Atlas of First Peoples*,
Robertson McCarta, London, 1990

Christopher Day, *Building with the Heart*, Green
Books, Devon, 1988

Christopher Day, *Places of the Soul*, Aquarian
Press, Thorsons, London, 1990

Charles Durrett and Kathryn McCamant, *Co-
Housing: A Contemporary Approach to Housing
Ourselves*, Ten Speed Press, California, 1988

Expo 2000, *The Hannover Principles: Design for
Sustainability*, William McDonough Architects,
New York, 1992

Farallones Institute, The Integral Urban House,
Sierra Club Books, San Francisco, California, 1979

Hassan Fathy, *Natural Energy and Vernacular
Architecture*, University of Chicago Press, 1986

Hassan Fathy, *Architecture for the Poor: An
Experiment in Rural Egypt*, University of Chicago
Press, 1973

Friends of Kebyar Vol 11.1 No 55 Jan-May 1993,
Portland Oregon - Anniversary Issue: The
Architecture of Bart Prince

Herbert Girardet, *The Gaia Atlas of Cities*, Anchor
Doubleday, New York; Gaia Books, London 1993

Mark Hammons, *The Architecture of Arthur
Dyson*, published in conjunction with the Fresno
Art Museum, California, 1993

Peter Harper, Chris Madsen, and Jeremy Light,
The Natural Garden Book, Simon & Schuster,
New York; Gaia Books, London 1994

Hasan-Uddin Khan, *Charles Correa*, A Mimar
Book, Butterworth Architecture, London, 1989

Index

Robert Kourik, *Designing and Maintaining Your Edible Landscape Naturally*, Metamorphic Press, Santa Rosa, California, 1986

James Lovelock, *Gaia: the Practical Science of Planetary Medicine*, Gaia, London, 1992

Reginald and Gladys Lubin, *The Indian Tipi*, Balantine, New York, 1985

Debra Lynn-Dadd, *Non-Toxic, Natural & Earthwise*, Jeremy Tarcher, Los Angeles, 1990

Christopher Mead, *Houses by Bart Prince*, University of New Mexico Press, Albuquerque, 1991

Bill Mollison and David Holmgren, *Permaculture*, Vols 1 & 2, Tagari, Stanley, Tasmania, 1979

Peter Nabakov and Robert Easton, *Native American Architecture*, Oxford University Press, New York, 1989

National Audubon Society, *Building Audubon House*, J Wiley, New York, 1994

John G Neihardt, *Black Elk Speaks*, Abacus, London, 1974

Victor Papanek, *Design for the Real World*, Thames & Hudson, London, 1985

David Pearson, *The Natural House Book*, Fireside Simon & Schuster, New York; Conran Octopus, London; Harper Collins, Sydney, Australia, 1989

Richard Register, *Ecocity Berkeley: Building Cities for a Healthy Future*, North Atlantic Books, Berkeley, California, 1987

Michael Reynolds, *Earthships*, Vols 1 and 2, Solar Survival Architecture, Taos, New Mexico, 1990, 1991

Paolo Soleri, *Arcology: The City in the Image of Man*, MIT Press, Cambridge, Massachusetts, 1969

H J Spinden (translator), *Songs of the Tewa*, Sunstone Press, Santa Fe, 1976

John and Nancy Jack Todd, *Bioshelters, Ocean Arks, City Farming: Ecology as a Basis of Design*, Sierra Club Books, San Francisco, California, 1984

Brenda and Robert Vale, *The Autonomous House*, Thames & Hudson, London, 1975

Brenda and Robert Vale, *Green Architecture*, Thames & Hudson, London, 1991

Carol Venolia, *Healing Environments*, Celestial Arts, California, 1988

Malcolm Wells, *Gentle Architecture*, McGraw-Hill, New York, 1982

Kees Zoeteman, *Gaia-Sophia: A Framework for Ecology*, Floris Books, Edinburgh, 1991

Glossary

Words that have been italicized on first mention in the main text are explained below.

adobe a mixture of earth, straw, and water used for making unbaked earth bricks.

anthroposophy the spiritual and mystical teachings of Rudolf Steiner, which many believe are psychologically valuable.

badgir an Egyptian wind scoop, into which wind can flow from several directions.

bahay kubo a typical Filipino bamboo house raised above the ground.

Baubiologie the science of the holistic interaction between life and the living environment.

cogon a long thin grass which is gathered and bundled together to form the thatch roof of the Filipino bahay kubo house.

co-housing developed by the residents themselves, co-housing combines the autonomy of private dwellings with the advantages of shared facilities and communal living.

disaggregate dividing architectural forms into a series of separate but interdependent volumes, common in India.

ecosystem a whole community, made up of living and non-living parts, and the flows of energy and materials between these parts.

eurythmy harmonious movements of the body to the rhythm of the spoken word.

feng shui the ancient Taoist art and science of auspicious siting and layout of buildings.

Gaia Theory the theory of James Lovelock which sees the Earth as a self-sustaining system where the evolution of organisms is closely coupled to the evolution of the environment. Self-regulation of climate and chemical composition are emergent properties of the Gaian system.

Gaiasophy a term coined by Kees Zoeteman, which describes the earth, Gaia, as a living organism, made up of components which can be compared to human organs. In order to understand this, you need to have wisdom (*sophia*) as well as knowledge.

hypocaust a heating system whereby heat from a furnace is channelled under the floor.

long barrow Neolithic burial mounds.

malqaf wind scoop. See also badgir.

nipa a type of palm whose leaves when sewn together form an alternative roof for the Filipino bahay kubo house.

tukod an awning-type window fixed in an open position in a traditional Filipino house.

ACKNOWLEDGEMENTS

Photographic Credits

All photographs are by the author except for the following: p.20 Chris Day; p.23 Durston Saylor; pp.24-5 Scot Zimmerman; p.64 Ton Alberts and M van Huut; pp.66-7 Bart Prince and Robert Reck; pp.68-9 Alan Weintraub; p.79 Carol Venolia; pp.80-1 Solar Survival Architecture; p.91 Gaia Group; pp.92-3 Paul Leech; p.94 Colin Wishart; pp.125, 126-7 Howard Liddell; pp.128-9 Francisco Mañosa; pp.130-1 Charles Correa; p.146 Kjell Wihlborg; p.149 Frederica Miller; p.153 Malcolm Wells; p.154 Reinhard Kanuka-Fuchs; p.155 Sydney Baggs.

Illustration Credits

All illustrations by the author except drawing on p.147 by Bill Mastin.

Author's Acknowledgements

First, I would like to thank the team at Gaia Books, in particular Bridget Morley for the beautiful design style and inspired picture selection, and Michele Staple for her patient and thorough editorial work. Also warm thanks to the rest of the production team: Susan Walby, Patrick Nugent, Pip Morgan, Suzy Boston, Kate McNulty, Cristina Masip, and, of course, to my wife Joss for all the fascinating discussions and her constant support throughout the project. I would also like to thank all those who supplied information and photographs of their work, helped comment on the draft text, and assisted with my travels: the Aga Khan Trust for Culture, Hans and Sonja Allback, Sydney Baggs, Stefan Bartha, Paul Bierman-Lytle, Varis Bokalders, Kirsten Childs, Charles Correa, Guy Dauncey, Arthur Dyson, David Easton, the Gaia Group, James Hubbell, Ross and Hildur Jackson, Reinhard Kanuka-Fuchs, Dr Carol Krinsky, Paul Leech, Howard Liddell, Max Lindegger, Francisco Mañosa, Bill McDonough, Bart Prince, Richard Register, Mike Reynolds, Julia Sarlós, Mariann Simon, Lazlo Szeker, Katherine Tiddens, and Carol Venolia.

Also published by Gaia Books

The Natural Garden Book
Peter Harper, Jeremy Light and Chris Madsen
£18.99 Hardback
ISBN 1 85675 085 X
This book puts gardening in its wider context. It is a fresh, practical and inspiring guide to creating a productive, healthy garden.

The Gaia Atlas of Cities
Herbert Girardet
£9.99
ISBN 1 85675 065 5
The Gaia Atlas of Cities explores the designs and styles that suit city dwellers yet at the same time sustain the support system of the living world.

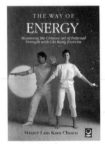

The Way of Energy
Master Lam Kam Chuen
£10.99
ISBN 1 85675 020 5
The first comprehensive guide to the most powerful form of the Chinese exercise system Chi Kung: Zhan Zhuang, or "standing like a tree".

The Book of Sound Therapy
Olivea Dewhurst-Maddock
£8.99
ISBN 1 85675 006 X
An authoritative introduction to the healing powers of sound, including the whole range of practical techniques used in sound therapy.

Eco Yoga
Henryk Skolimowski
£10.99
ISBN 1 85675 071 X
Yoga exercises for the mind. Practices and meditations for a new relationship between the mind, body and planet.

The Book of Colour Healing
Theo Gimbel
£8.99
ISBN 1 85675 026 4
A practical guide to the impact of colour on your health, and how to use coloured treatment lamps to heal ailments.

For a catalogue of titles published by Gaia Books, write or telephone Gaia Books, 20 High Street, Stroud, Gloucestershire, GL5 1AS.
Tel 01453 752985
Fax 01453 752987